WRITING LIGHT VERSE
and
PROSE HUMOR

RICHARD ARMOUR

//

Writing Light Verse and Prose Humor

BOSTON

THE WRITER, INC.

PUBLISHERS

PN
1042
.A7
1971

Library of Congress Catalog Card Number: 77–142595
ISBN: 0–87116–064–1

ACKNOWLEDGMENTS

GRATEFUL acknowledgment is made to the authors, publishers, and others listed below for permission to include the following poems:

"A Ballade of Suicide," from *The Collected Poems of G. K. Chesterton*, copyright by Dodd, Mead & Company, 1911, 1932. Reprinted by permission of Dodd, Mead & Company.

"The Female of the Species Is Hardier than the Male," from *Husbands Are Difficult*, by Phyllis McGinley. Published by Duell, Sloan & Pearce, Inc., copyright 1941 by Phyllis McGinley. Reprinted by permission of Duell, Sloan & Pearce, Inc.

Lines from "certain maxims of archy," from *archy and mehitabel*, by Don Marquis, copyright 1927 by Doubleday & Co., Inc. Reprinted by permission of Doubleday & Co., Inc.

"On the Vanity of Earthly Greatness," from *Gaily the Troubadour*, by Arthur Guiterman, published and copyright 1936 by E. P. Dutton & Co., Inc., New York. Reprinted by permission of E. P. Dutton & Co., Inc.

First stanza of "The Legend of the First Cam-U-el," from *Lyric Laughter*, by Arthur Guiterman, published and copyright 1939 by E. P. Dutton & Co., Inc., New York. Reprinted by permission of E. P. Dutton & Co., Inc.

Lines from *Conversation at Midnight*, by Edna St. Vincent Millay, published by Harper & Brothers, copyright

1937 by Edna St. Vincent Millay. Reprinted by permission
of Brandt & Brandt.

"The Lady Is Cold," from *The Lady Is Cold,* by E. B.
White, published by Harper & Brothers. Reprinted by permission of the author and Harper & Brothers.

"Lord Finchley," from *Cautionary Tales,* by Hilaire Belloc, copyright by Alfred A. Knopf, Inc., New York. Published in England by Gerald Duckworth & Company, Ltd.
Reprinted by permission of Alfred A. Knopf, Inc.

"Song of the Open Road," from *The Face Is Familiar,*
by Ogden Nash. Copyright 1931, 1933, 1935, 1936, 1937,
1938, 1939, 1940, by Ogden Nash. Reprinted by permission
of Little, Brown & Company.

Lines from *Poems in Praise of Practically Nothing,* by
Samuel Hoffenstein, published by Liveright Publishing
Corporation. Reprinted by permission of Liveright Pub-
lishing Corporation.

"A Stropshire Lad," from *Bay Window Ballads,* by
David McCord, copyright, 1935, by Charles Scribner's
Sons. Used by permission of the publishers, Charles Scrib-
ner's Sons.

"The Lazy Writer," from *Poems,* by Bert Leston Taylor,
published by Alfred A. Knopf, Inc. Reprinted by permission of Emma B. Taylor.

Poems by Arthur Guiterman, James Norman Hall, and
E. B. White that first appeared in *The New Yorker.* Re-
printed by permission of the authors and The New Yorker
Magazine, Inc. and acknowledged on reverse of title page.

My thanks are due also to the editors and publishers of
the following for their cooperation in permitting me to
reprint certain of my poems which originally appeared in
their pages: *The Atlantic Monthly, The American Legion*

Magazine, Better Homes and Gardens, The Christian Science Monitor, Collier's, Cosmopolitan, Country Gentleman, D.A.C. News, Good Housekeeping, Judge, Look, The New Leader, The New Yorker, New York Herald Tribune, Redbook, The Saturday Evening Post, The Saturday Review, Today's Health, The Wall Street Journal, and *Woman's Home Companion,* also Bruce Humphries, Inc. (publishers of *Yours for the Asking* and *Privates' Lives*), Beechhurst Press, Inc. (publishers of *Leading With My Left* and *Golf Bawls*), Harper & Bros. (publishers of *For Partly Proud Parents*), and McGraw-Hill Book Company, Inc. (publishers of *Light Armour* and *Nights With Armour*).

CONTENTS

FOREWORD

I WAS not sure whether I should call this a foreword or put it in the back of the book and call it a backword. I was not even sure whether I should put it in the book at all. But since the history of this book is a little complicated, I thought I should add a few words of explanation.

Originally called *Writing Light Verse,* this book was first published in 1947 and became the first and only "how to" book in its field, which it still is. One advantage of this is that it enables me to call it the best, as I frequently do.

Eleven years later, in 1958, I revised and updated the book. Since books, like people, have a way of growing old and being forgotten, I thought that would be the end of it. I felt that if the second edition should live as long as the first, that would mean a total life span of over twenty years, fully as hard for a book to achieve as for a man to reach a hundred.

But the book is still alive, and I hope lively. Just to make sure, however, it has been given a word transfusion. Not only has the basic text been checked and updated again, but chapters have been added that give at least the fundamentals of writing prose humor. These additional chapters enlarge the scope of the book, by discussing prose writing as well as light verse, though humor remains the common element.

Or perhaps I should say the uncommon element, because the writing of humor requires a certain attitude toward life (and especially toward oneself), a sensitivity to words, and a willingness to write and revise, write and revise. But it is worth it. Comedy, I think, is as high an art as tragedy. It is as important to make people laugh as to make people cry. Whether you try writing humor in verse or in prose, I wish you well.

R.A.

WRITING LIGHT VERSE
and
PROSE HUMOR

CHAPTER ONE

On Purpose

THERE are books on how to do just about anything. You can find one on how to build a birdhouse, twirl a baton, win an argument, operate an abacus, remember names and faces, grow tuberous begonias, or play a shepherd's pipe. But, while there are a number of books on how to write a novel, a play, a short story, or a serious poem, there is little designed to help the writer of light verse and prose humor —perhaps because writing humor seems so simple that help is not considered necessary. Certainly there is no dearth of persons trying to write it. Magazines receive great quantities of humor in verse and prose. Most of these writings, however, fall short of publishable quality, so editors continually look for more, hoping to get even a few really funny pieces to offer their readers.

There is a larger and higher-paying market for light verse than for serious poetry, and prose humor is always in short supply. Editors are always in the market for something that will lighten and brighten an issue. This is true even of top-circulation magazines which pay the highest rates. Writing salable humor depends on good technique, and technique is something that can be studied and learned. In this book, technique will be emphasized, though there will also be suggestions about such essentials as subject matter and attitude.

Many have been misled by the apparent ease of writing humor and have entered the lists with high hopes, only to withdraw, chagrined and perplexed, after the eighth or tenth rejection slip. Others have scored a few times, but have been unable to keep it up; or have achieved their success only in some local, small-paying publication. This book is intended to encourage all of these persons to intensify their efforts, and to give them guidance in writing about the right subjects in the right way and sending their product to the right markets. It is, frankly, another of the host of "How to —" books. As such, it is meant to be simple and practical, a stimulus to do and a help in the doing. If something faintly resembling literary criticism is occasionally involved, it is only because it behooves the writer of humor to know the difference between bad and good, and between fair and first-rate. Nor can the psychology of editors and readers be wholly neglected.

The first part of this book will deal with light verse. I shall illustrate the various technical points with selections from my own verses, for two reasons. In the first place, I know these poems of mine—how they were worked up and worked over—better than I do the poems of any other writer. And in the second place, I confess a sort of parental partiality for my own poems, homely as many of these

verse children may be. To quote from myself without further apology:

EXCEPTION

I do not care for forward brats
Or barking dogs or mangy cats
Or filthy old fedora hats,
    Unless they're mine.

I do not care for easy morals
Or family or other quarrels
Or stamps or coins or shells or corals,
    Unless they're mine.

I do not care for public kisses
Or haughty looks or sneers or hisses
Or even poems such as this is,
    Unless they're mine.

Or, in lines that are equally appropriate:

FAVORITE

That poem is a splendid thing,
    I love to hear you quote it.
I like the thought, I like the swing,
    I like it all. (I wrote it.)

This does not mean, I hasten to say, that I do not also like
what others write. Actually I like their writings all the
more because, from personal experience, I know what effort went into them. I can appreciate, as I could not if I had
not myself tried so hard to do the same sort of thing, the
author's satisfaction at having discovered and exploited a
new subject or given an original turn to an old one. Time

and again I find myself sighing inwardly, "I wish I had thought of that. I wish I had written that." But, happily, envy soon changes to honest admiration, which in turn transmutes itself into emulation, the urgent desire to do as well. And this is at once a stimulus to jump again over the poetic bar and a prompting to raise it to a new height. Competition is keen in the writing of light verse, as in everything else. One can recognize and even rejoice in this fact without losing regard and hope for one's own work.

What are some of the things the light verse writer needs to know if he is to practice the art or craft satisfyingly and successfully? He should know what to write about: which subjects lend themselves to treatment in light verse and which do not. He should know how to start out, how to break the white virginity of a piece of blank paper. He should know the metrical forms that are most effective for this type of writing, and how to handle them with facility and grace. He should know the uses and abuses of rhyme, and be able to distinguish the fresh and interesting from the hackneyed. He should know how to begin a piece of verse in such a way as to attract attention and arouse antici-pation, and how to close it with force or unexpectedness. He should know when he has said enough and when there is more to be said; in other words, when it would weaken his poem to add details or to reiterate, and when his poem would be weak without some expansion. He should be able to recognize, and concoct, an effective title. He should know how, through revision, to hide the joints and seams, the evidence of effort and strain; how to give, finally, the effect of naturalness and sudden inspiration. He should know what are the magazine and newspaper markets for light verse, and which are most appropriate for (and therefore most likely purchasers of) his product. He should know about timing—the latest date, for example, that he should submit to a monthly magazine a poem on returning Christmas gifts, on carving the Thanksgiving turkey, or on viewing the Easter parade. He should know the form of manuscript that editors like, the significance of a personal note instead of a rejection slip, whether he needs a literary agent, and a good many other things.

But first he should know what light verse is, and what are its many varieties, if this is the kind of writing to which he intends to devote himself.

CHAPTER TWO

Putting the Light on It

AT the outset let me express my opinion, however debatable it may be, that light verse is poetry. That is to say, it is a type of poetry instead of a distinct art of its own. It may differ considerably from other poetry, but the difference is chiefly in approach or attitude, and then often only in degree. The light verse writer therefore is, or is capable of being, more than a mere versifier. He is a poet, although there may be a twinkle instead of a contemplative look in his eye, and he may keep his hair cut as short as that of a businessman. Consequently, I shall make so bold as to use "a piece of light verse" and "poem" interchangeably, and shall not hesitate to call a writer of light verse, especially if he is a good one, a poet.

Even when it is bad, light verse is poetry of a sort. Then, of course, it is bad poetry. If there is a large proportion of light verse that is pretty terrible, the reason is that much of it is undertaken haphazardly, written without proper

6

literary standards, and displayed to friends and editors before it is fully ready. The writer of serious poetry is more
likely to know the difficulties that must be overcome. He is
also inclined to try a little harder and to take a little more
pride in the effort. If the light verse writer will consider
himself also a poet, with at least some of the poet's respon-
sibilities, he may raise his standards and be dissatisfied with
casual and shoddy workmanship. In this event, he can be
sure that the editors and publishers will become more hos-
pitable.

When it is really good, light verse is quite respectable.
Although usually in the odd corners and inconspicuous
places, it is published in the same magazines that publish
the prose of distinguished authors. It is reprinted in anthologies and enshrined in Bartlett's *Familiar Quotations*.
It is memorized by schoolchildren, studied and commented
on by critics, read over the radio, and set to music. It has
universality, and is translated into other languages. It has
permanence, and is passed along and enjoyed by succeeding
generations. The Greeks and Romans wrote it. Chaucer
wrote it. Shakespeare wrote it. It was the favorite form of
that greatest and most prolific of ancient and modern writers, Anon., for it has a folk element and is decidedly of the
people. It is extremely popular in our own pleasure-loving,
fun-poking day.

No definition, particularly a brief one, is likely to be
completely satisfactory. But here is one that is broad
enough to take everything in, including perhaps some
things that do not belong in. *Light verse is poetry written
in the spirit of play*. This does not mean that it is, or should
be, undertaken and accomplished casually. Once-over-
lightly is not the idea. As I shall try to make plain, light

verse frequently demands more precision, more fastidious-
ness of technique, than poetry of other and greater kinds.
It is highly artful, much though it may strive to hide its art.
What distinguishes it, however, is the playful attitude of
the poet. Whether the mood is gay or satirical, whimsical
or witty, the writer of light verse usually appears to be having a good time. If he is writing satire, he may have a bit of
reform in view. But he does not permit his "message" to
weigh too heavily upon him; nor does he count too much
on being successful in effecting social improvement.

Usually the light verse writer wishes to amuse. Oliver
Wendell Holmes recognized this desire, and playfully exaggerated his own considerable powers, in *The Height of
the Ridiculous:*

> I wrote some lines once on a time
> In wondrous merry mood,
> And thought, as usual, men would say
> They were exceeding good.
>
> They were so queer, so very queer,
> I laughed as I would die;
> Albeit, in a general way,
> A sober man am I.
>
> I called my servant, and he came;
> How kind it was of him
> To mind a slender man like me,
> He of the mighty limb!
>
> "These to the printer," I exclaimed,
> And in my humorous way
> I added (as a trifling jest),
> "There'll be the devil to pay."

He took the paper, and I watched,
　　And saw him peep within;
At the first line he read, his face
　　Was all upon the grin.

He read the next; the grin grew broad,
　　And shot from ear to ear;
He read the third; a chuckling noise
　　I now began to hear.

The fourth; he broke into a roar;
　　The fifth; his waistband split;
The sixth; he burst five buttons off,
　　And tumbled in a fit.

Ten days and nights, with sleepless eye,
　　I watched that wretched man,
And since, I never dare to write
　　As funny as I can.

Most of us write as funny as we can, and only regret that
it is not funnier. The death rate from excessive laughter is
very low. As a matter of fact, light verse is more likely to
elicit a slight smile, or merely a pleased sensation inside,
than to provoke a guffaw. This is because light verse at its
best has subtlety and overtones of meaning rather than
complete obviousness, although it must always be clear.
Like good serious poetry, it is not exhausted at first reading. One is amused by its thought or intrigued by its expression each time one returns to it. Thus Hilaire Belloc's
epitaph on the unfortunate Lord Finchley is not laugh-
provoking. But the reader does get a quiet sort of amusement from these lines:

> Lord Finchley tried to mend the Electric Light
> Himself. It struck him dead: And serve him right!
> It is the business of the wealthy man
> To give employment to the artisan.

As I have discovered from reading this poem many times, it cannot be worn out. The indignant rather than sympathetic treatment of this well-meaning gentleman's demise is repeatedly amusing. The conciseness of the two-line narrative and its unexpected moral is always something to admire. There is also the desire to read it aloud to someone else, which is another sure sign of good light verse.

Much light verse is not funny at all. It may simply be gay and lilting: the poet at play with words and music. Consider almost any of Shakespeare's songs. This one, for instance:

> Sigh no more, ladies, sigh no more;
>   Men were deceivers ever;
> One foot in sea and one on shore,
>   To one thing constant never.
>   Then sigh not so,
>   But let them go,
> And be you blithe and bonny,
> Converting all your sounds of woe
> Into Hey nonny, nonny.

This is light verse, according to our broad definition. It is near the peak of playful gaiety, but not what you are likely to sell today. Magazine editors require less music (though a good lilt will sometimes help) but more point and twist, compressed into relatively few lines for the busy reader.

Humorous verse is easier to sell, these days, than serious poetry, and it generally pays better. This may not be justice, poetic or otherwise, but it is a fact. For examples of the type of light verse that is presently salable, as well as of lasting value, I refer the reader to *What Cheer* (also available as *The Pocket Book of Humorous Verse*), a wide-ranging anthology of humorous and witty verse edited by David McCord, himself an able practitioner of the art. In his informative and graceful introduction, the editor states that his test for inclusion in the volume is the affirmative answer to "Is it funny? Is it witty?" But he cautions that this is not enough, for the verse must also be "well turned and technically sound." Still other examples of humorous verse will be found in various collections and anthologies, such as Charles Preston's *The Light Touch,* from the "Pepper and Salt" column in *The Wall Street Journal*; the small *Anthology of Light Verse,* edited by Louis Kronenberger; that all-inclusive anthology, *The Silver Treasury of Light Verse,* edited by Oscar Williams, containing "poems of wit, ribaldry, fun and foibles" from Chaucer to Ogden Nash; and the more specialized and selective volume, *The New Yorker Book of Verse,* marked by sophistication and expert craftsmanship. Also, of course, the various collections of such hardy perennials among light verse writers as Phyllis McGinley, Dorothy Parker, Margaret Fishback, and Ogden Nash. Many of these books are available in paperback, as well as in the public library.

Before I go into detail, let me discuss a little further the breadth and variety of light verse. It is precisely because it appears in so many guises that I have been compelled, despite some misgivings, to include it under the general heading of poetry. Narrowly defined, it might—although with considerable difficulty and the admission of many borderline cases—be set apart as a distinct type. Considered broadly, however, it becomes inextricably intermingled with poetry of other kinds.

In content, light verse ranges from the nonsense rhymes of Edward Lear and Lewis Carroll to the meaningful commentaries on the politics and society of the day that Dryden, Pope, and Byron wrote in the seventeenth, eighteenth, and nineteenth centuries and that in the present century has been written by such penetrating satirists as A. P. Herbert and others in *Punch,* and more recently by Marya Mannes. In technique, it ranges from the simple play-rhymes of children, like

> First's the worst,
>   Second's the same,
> Last's the best
>   Of all the game,

to such exercises in metrical facility as the lyrics of W. S. Gilbert and the nimble verses of Berton Braley and Arthur Guiterman. For instance, the latter's well-known piece about the camel, that opens:

> Across the sands of Syria,
>   Or, possibly, Algeria,
> Or some benighted neighborhood of barrenness and drouth,
>   There came the prophet Sam-u-el
>   Upon the Only Cam-u-el,
> A bumpy, grumpy quadruped of discontented mouth.

In mood, it ranges from the quiet contentment of Thomas Hood in *The Cigar:*

Some sigh for this and that;
   My wishes don't go far;
The world may wag at will,
   So I have my cigar. . . .

I do not seek for fame,
   A General with a scar;
A private let me be,
   So I have my cigar. . . .

The ardent flame of love
   My bosom cannot char;
I smoke, but do not burn,
   So I have my cigar. . . .

(and so on through many stanzas), to the annoyed attitude
of the anonymous "old fogy" who wrote:

I'm thankful that the sun and moon
   Are both hung up so high
That no presumptuous hand can stretch
   And pull them from the sky.
If they were not, I have no doubt
   But some reforming ass
Would recommend to take them down
   And light the world with gas.

Morally, one might add, it ranges from innocent nursery
rhymes to unprintable limericks.

Certainly light verse is no narrow or small thing. To
W. H. Auden, who takes a very inclusive view of it in his
introduction to *The Oxford Book of Light Verse,* it is all
the poetry which is "simple, clear, and gay." And Auden
has written that kind as well as some to which these adjec-

tives are not so surely applicable. At any rate, light verse is poetry in many moods and forms. It includes nonsense verse, epigrams, comic epitaphs, humorous narrative poems, limericks, metrical trickery in such forms as the triolet, roundel, and ballade, satirical verse, and parodies. It has been written by some poets, like Frederick Locker-Lampson, C. S. Calverley, and Guy Wetmore Carryl, who specialized in it, as well as by a great many serious poets, like Browning, Byron, Edwin Arlington Robinson, Robert Frost, and T. S. Eliot, who were human enough not to be deadly serious all the time. Even such reputedly humorless and unbending poets as Milton and Wordsworth had a few flings at it, although without notable success.

However, light verse of the kind for which one can find a market today can safely be limited to what is called *vers de societé:* humorous or witty verse that comments critically on contemporary life. It is usually to some degree funny. It is often, if not always, satirical. It delights in superficialities and in the absurd and incongruous. It deftly touches upon human weaknesses in the individual, in groups of individuals, and in mankind at large. It holds the mirror up to nature at times when nature is off guard or doing something foolish. The mirror, too, is likely to be a bit convex or concave, like the ones in a Fun House at the beach, so that nature's deformities and eccentricities are exaggerated. Playful as the poet is, he may very well be unsparing in his ridicule of the ridiculous, his deflation of the inflated. To achieve his end, he uses every device of verse and language at his command: dancing meter, unusual rhymes, unexpected turns of thought, similes, puns, and all the rest. He calls upon his ingenuity and resourcefulness to find new subjects or to treat in a surprising or at least refreshing manner those that have been dealt with many times before. The poet is at play, but he often gets and gives considerable mental exercise before the game is done.

CHAPTER THREE

Getting the Idea

"LIFE," says Newman Levy in his *Song for the Nearest Riveting Machine*, "is a poem by Dorothy Parker." In any event, life is what Dorothy Parker wrote about in her poems, and what others who would write poems at all comparable to hers should also write about. For light verse, if not actually life itself, has the qualities of life. It is lively and lifelike.

In seeking ideas and material for light verse, one can do no better than to look long and intently at life, which means mostly at people. There is the stuff of light verse in every aspect of people: how they look, how they think, how they act (as infants, as adolescents, in middle age), how they woo and wed, how they earn a living, how they play, how they eat and drink, how they elect and govern one another. Even how, and especially why, they make war. If people were invariably practical and reasonable, there

would be little here for the light verse writer, who thrives
upon stupidity, inconsistency, and comedies of errors. But
fortunately for him at least, people are delightfully impractical and unreasonable a large part of the time. So long as
there are people, he need not fear a dearth of subject matter.

It is fortunate also that people, often with the same shortcomings, are the amused readers of what is written about
others. They take pleasure in recognizing in themselves
such small faults as they will admit, and in recognizing and
feeling superior to the incredible stupidities of others. Furthermore, the writer himself is of the same species. In hold-
ing the mirror up to nature he has only to gaze into the
looking glass. He is at once an excellent source of material
and, allowing for personal partiality, a capable critic of his
own handling of it. If, however, he is neither self-critical
nor willing to display and make fun of his own weaknesses,
he cuts himself out of a wealth of subject matter. Likewise
he foregoes the most ingratiating approach that is open to
him. For people like to have human foibles pointed out,
but they quite naturally do not like the finger thrust directly at them. They prefer to catch the similarity and
make the personal application by themselves. That is why
it is well, when writing about the shortcomings of people,
often to write, or appear to write, about yourself. Only be
sure that the fault you are describing is not one peculiar to
you. For then the reader would fail to recognize or appreciate it, and you would be forced to keep it to yourself
(i.e. unpublished) as a personal joke. In other words, make
of yourself as horrible an example as you like, but be certain that you are really an example and not an exception.
This caution cannot be too often repeated. Test your sub-

ject carefully for the breadth of its application, the universality of its appeal.

As a source of subject matter, consider the human body, the body unbeautiful. Think of it from every angle and in every connection. Think not of how admirably conceived, how efficient and durable it is, but how much better it might have been, how ineffective it is under certain circumstances, and how frequently it gets out of shape and out of fix. Ideas for verses are there, and will shortly become apparent. Let me demonstrate with a few of the dozens of poems I have myself written about just one small item in this category, human hair. There is no better laboratory for poems on this subject than the barber shop, where there is ample leisure while waiting or being worked upon and where the rhythmical snip of the barber's shears establishes a metrical pattern. Morris Bishop, in *The Tales the Barbers Tell,* has written the light verse classic with a barber shop locale. In a scene of "hushed and haughty barbers cutting each other's hair" after the day's work is over, a barber narrates the dreadful story of the time he gave a customer the works, from the Special Egg Gasoline Shampoo to the ultimate tar facial and oil-and-vinegar hair dressing. What gave the writer his idea was probably a study of the long list of services the barber is prepared to render, as well as recurrent invitations to more than the desired haircut, whispered insistently into his ear. For my own part, I have found material for poems in the futility of instructing barbers, with minds already made up, as to how one's hair is to be cut; in the endless reduplication of one's image when the mirrors reflect each other in just the right way; and in the apparently wasteful disposition of the sweepings. My treatment of the last runs as follows:

Hair Today, Gone Tomorrow

I wonder why there's nothing done
  With all the human hair
That slowly sifts and falls in drifts
  Beside the barber's chair,

That gravitates like winter's snow
  And with as little noise—
The childish curls of little girls,
  The stubborn spikes of boys,

The heavy locks of manly men
  That sink in lanky parcels,
The tiny trim of bald-pates' rim
  That flutters down in morsels,

The black, the brown, the in-between,
  The blonde, the red, the hoar
That slowly waft from up aloft
  And settle on the floor.

By-products there must surely be,
  If modern men of science
Will sagely view the residue
  Left by the barber's clients.

Oh, must it all be swept away,
  Can't someone put a stop
To throwing out what's just about
  Man's only home-grown crop?

More thought on the subject of hair, with observation of
the greater imaginativeness and resourcefulness of women,
led me to write such a piece as this:

CROWNING GLORY

No trick of magician we've seen can compare
With the wonders a woman can work with her hair.
The elegant damsel who dazzles the eye
In her evening coiffure swept up gorgeously high
Gets scarcely a glance from the male over yonder
Next day when her hair is let straggle and wander.
A garland of ringlets, and presto! one thinks
That here is a giddy, impractical minx;
But the masculine trim of a businesslike bob
Turns her into the sort who could hold any job.
A face-framing cluster of flattering tresses
Brings out all the glamour the lady possesses.
A bun or a braid makes her look rather quaint,
Which maybe she is and then maybe she ain't.

While a woman thus alters her looks with her hair-do
And tries every sort of both common and rare do,
To the end of his days, as he youthfully started,
A man wears his hair either straight back or parted.

To illustrate the fact that it is possible to shift one's point
of view rather abruptly, and also that one poem will very
often suggest the writing of another, I cite this one, which
came to me after a little toying with the word "hair-do" in
the foregoing:

HAIR LINES

A thought I might further pursue,
    But, being a gentleman, won't,
Is that many a woman's hair-do
    Might better be termed a hair-don't.

From a man's point of view, the most vexing thing about hair is the way, year after year, the handsome youthful head of it becomes ever sparser—an index to age and a barometer of romantic appeal. There is a verse epigram in this, when the idea is mulled over and the words and phrases are pushed around a bit:

DEPRECIATING INTEREST

A man always meets
  With fewer side glances
As his hairline retreats
  And his waistline advances.

A little more cogitation on receding hairlines, with personal applications, yields:

HEAD START

I note with dismay
  And each year with more sorrow
That my scalp of today
  Is my forehead tomorrow.

An idea may also be gained by observing the vain (in more senses than one) attempts of a man to conceal his lack of hair, for instance the way he combs his few remaining strands over the bald spot, or how he acts in public. In elevators, for example:

ON AND OFF

In elevators it's not mere
Politeness or its lack, I fear,
That governs, as one goes aloft,
Which hats stay on, and which are doffed.

> For men whose hair is nice and thick
> Take off their hats at double quick,
> While those whose hair is not so hardy
> Are apt to be a little tardy.

I have no notion of how many poems about hair I have written, and sold. But I do know that I have not exhausted the subject.

The other parts of the body are just about as good as subject matter. There is the nose, for instance. How few the noses that are the right size and shape! And yet in how prominent a place this feature is situated, where it cannot be concealed by either hair or clothing. Or the teeth. Give a thought to the adolescent and his braces, the dentist's drill (and his even more terrifying bill), the incredibly even and lustrous incisors of the movie star. James Norman Hall, the novelist, once did a nice piece on the latter subject for *The New Yorker*. It is only a pity that subsequent generations of movie-goers, who missed the elder Douglas Fairbanks on the screen, will not enjoy it quite so much as some of the rest of us.

REFLECTIONS ON DOUGLAS FAIRBANKS

[After Having Seen Him in the Flesh, at Tahiti]

> Are the teeth, so dazzling white,
> Bared in the well-known grin at night?
> Does he wear it when alone?
> Is it now so much his own
> That he cannot, if he would,
> Alter it in any mood?
>
> It must be so. A face will bear
> Only so much constant wear;

Then it takes a final shape
From which there can be no escape.

Woe to him who is possessed
Of a grin, though of the best!
Friends may die—his nearest kin:
Willy-nilly, he must grin.
Waking, sleeping, drunk or sober,
From October to October,
Without cause, or rhyme, or reason,
In, but mostly out of, season
On his poor abusèd face
Sits the grin he can't erase.

Movie aspirants, beware
How your perfect teeth you bare!
Let his face a warning be.
Grin, but not eternally.

A minor but perhaps more universal observation in connection with teeth is contained in the short piece that follows. It is an example of something that everyone has
probably thought about but that no one, so far as I know,
has troubled to put into verse.

Molar Dolors

Man's teeth were built
     For all their needs
Except to tilt
     With berry seeds.

I mentioned above that the light verse writer in search
of ideas might give a thought to the adolescent and braces.
One way of going at it would be to discuss the "zippered-
up" look of that mouth full of wires. Another, though it is

almost too depressing to write about, would be to consider the financial beating the parent takes. I tackled the latter subject, after a bitter personal experience, in these lines for *Good Housekeeping*:

LET'S GET THIS STRAIGHT

My daughter has an orthodontist
Around whom I appear my gauntest
And wear my suit that's worn and seedy,
In hope he'll class me with the needy.

Yet months from now, I have no doubt,
When bands are off and she goes out
With straightened teeth and gleaming glances,
I'll be in straitened circumstances.

Then there is the stomach. What a vast deal of humor there is in its inner doings and its outward bulge. The fact that we take its well-being so much for granted provoked me to this:

ANATOMICAL OBSERVATION

The stomach is, in every creature,
An interesting sort of feature:
When it works well, you're not aware
That you have any organ there,
But when it gets to working ill you
Are quite convinced it's going to kill you.

Which, again, is applicable to all but that rare individual who boasts that he has "never had a sick day in his life." (A statement so palpably untrue that it might also be played upon in a piece of light verse.)

Since it is, as I have said, not the body efficient but the body deficient that makes for humor in verse, there is a promising field in man's illnesses: the all-too-common cold, allergies, the unceasing and losing struggle with the sinuses, operations (minor when performed, major when discussed), doctors and nurses and hospitals, those half-filled bottles in the medicine chest that remind of past ailments, waiting out a quarantine, trying all the remedies thrust upon you by that distinguished specialist on all diseases and mishaps, your next-door neighbor, and the like. As long as doctors practice, poets can preach.

Enough of man as he is. Now for what he tries to look like by means of the clothing he wears. There is the clothing store, with its numerous company of handsome, impeccably dressed, and infinitely superior salesmen. There is the experience everyone has had of getting a rare and too-revealing view of oneself all around:

Undone with Mirrors

One mirror does not constitute
A vital threat to me,
But when I'm trying on a suit
And see myself in three,
I get a sudden full-length view
Of profile and of rear—
A sight I'm unaccustomed to
And which I always fear.

There is the struggle between the adventure of a flamboyant wide herringbone and the safety of a nondescript weave that is almost identical with the suit you are wearing. There is the temptation of the smart, snugly-fitting coat, and the realization that you haven't the figure for it. There

are all the vexing problems connected with ties, such as
what to do with the ghastly ones that well-meaning but
color-blind friends and relatives gave you for Christmas, or
how to tie them so that the two ends will be of equal length.
Then there are hats, from variously snapped snap brims to
the derbies and Homburgs of diplomats. And of course
shoes: what they do for, and to, the feet. But it is the clothes
of women that offer the greatest possibilities to the light
verse writer. For clothes may not make a man, but buying
them for his wife can just about break him. The size and
shape of women's hats is one constant inspiration. Another
is their cost, as well as the cost of gowns and accessories.
(There is probably a bit of verse in the curious fact that
the word "accessories" is applied both to women's clothing
and to automobiles.) To give an example, there is this way
of putting the economic aspect of this inexhaustible subject:

Designing Women

I know very little of dresses,
   And less, even less, about hats.
I'm the type of mere male who just guesses
   That fashion designers are bats.

One fact, though, I've known a long while is
   Consistent and sane and precise:
The more fantastic the style is,
   The more fantastic the price.

There is also the paradoxical way a woman dresses down as
she dresses up. The idea can be phrased like this:

Dressed for Eve

With evening gown backless and flimsy for fair,
  There was much, in her words, that had merit:
She said, with a sigh, she had nothing to wear,
  And darned if the gal didn't wear it!

Or something can be said of woman's winter hardihood—
cause for wonder and admiration by the well-swathed male.
If I am right, every man has noticed this instance of warm-
bloodedness. Or is it fortitude for the sake of fashion?

Bare Facts

Each winter I wonder, to put it quite simply,
Why girls with bare legs never get all goose pimply,
While merely to see them
Is enough to give me them!

Finally, give a thought to the satirical possibilities in a matter of common knowledge: how women of whatever age or
shape convince themselves that they will look exactly like
that gorgeous model if they wear the same outfit. Here is
one treatment of this many-faceted topic:

Beauty Before Age

A thing for which I do not care,
  Or count among aesthetic blisses,
Is seeing senior matrons wear
  The frocks designed for junior misses.

Another is this couplet which came to me while I was trying to hurry my wife past an exclusive shop. I sold it

for enough to buy her an inexpensive dress to wear around the house:

LADY SHOPPERS, BEWARE

Show-window manikins
Have slenderer fannykins.

Equally good material is latent in how women wobble around on high-heeled shoes that are a size smaller than their feet, how they think sixty dollars too much to pay for a dress but cannot be restrained from buying the same thing at the bargain price of $59.98. And so on.

This leads quite naturally to that richest of mother lodes for the light verse writer out prospecting for subject matter: the battle of the sexes. "Sex," as Louis Kronenberger asserts in his introduction to *An Anthology of Light Verse*, "is obviously one of the very few topics that have any paramount interest for mankind." There is no end to the humorous and satirical verses that can be written by men about women, by women about men, or by the writer about his or her own sex, always pointing up the special foibles that make a comparison of the sexes so fascinating to writer and reader alike. The male light verse writers, such as Samuel Hoffenstein and Arthur Guiterman, have done very well. But the women, notably Dorothy Parker, Phyllis McGinley, Margaret Fishback, Ethel Jacobson, and Georgie Starbuck Galbraith, have done even better. They seem to have a sharper eye—as well as a sharper pen. It is interesting to note that Edna St. Vincent Millay, writing in the manner of Ogden Nash and even referring to him by name, included an acid piece about her own sex in *Conversation at Midnight*. I refer to the passage wherein a group of men,

gathered one evening in a New York bachelor's apart-
ment, inevitably get around to the subject of women. One
of them, Pygmalion, having declared that "women are
poison," continues:

". . . As Ogden Nash might put it:
They're always wanting attention, and if you don't feel like
      kissing them every minute of the day it's a misdemeanour;
And right in the middle of the season they send your shooting-
      clothes to the cleanour."

And more in the same vein.

I have myself written a great many verses on the battle of
the sexes, and have taken both sides. An instance is this
little jibe at one of the weaknesses of women:

MAKEUP ARTISTS

Women, one finds,
Make up their minds,
Quarrels, and faces
In public places.

On the other hand, there is this to be said about the unfin-
ished adolescence so often displayed by the grown man:

RELAPSE

Boys will be boys,
And then again
Despite all their poise,
So, sometimes, will men.

This is also illustrative of something I shall discuss later:
how one can often get started on a poem by thinking about

some common saying or truism. In this case "boys will be boys" provided both the needed spark and the opening line.

Much, of a light-romantic sort, can be written about the sexes while the hunt is on. Any phase of the chase is good, so long as it is considered in an acerb rather than saccharine mood. Margaret Fishback is a specialist here. Despite the many poems she has already written on this theme, she may still be counted on to come up with many more. And invariably she contrives to be gay and critical in the proper proportions for light verse. Characteristic of her playful, delicately satiric approach to the subject of romance is her *To a Young Man Selecting Six Orchids,* with its repeated query of "Is she worth the price you pay?" With mock seriousness she warns the foolhardy young fellow of the train of dire consequences which the purchase of half a dozen orchids may set off: beginning with apparently harmless satin ribbons and culminating in such millstones of domesticity as leases, refrigerators, and sometimes, she warns, "even twins."

As an instance of the value of reading what others write, about which I shall have more to say in a subsequent chapter, I might note here that Margaret Fishback's poem about the young man and the orchids elicited from me a poem on a related subject. With her gift-bearing beau in mind, I wrote the following:

LINES FOR A YOUNG MAN GOING CALLING

Chocolates add pounds, you know,
    Orchids quickly wilt,
Silver gadgets tarnish so,
    Gold is often gilt.

> Hose wear out, and furs for some
> Months lie on the shelf.
> So, my darling, I shall come
> Bringing just myself.

While I am paying debts, I must confess that I was assisted in the above by a recollection of Samuel Hoffenstein's *Poems in Praise of Practically Nothing,* specifically the well-known lines:

> You buy some flowers for your table;
> You tend them tenderly as you're able;
> You fetch them water from hither and thither—
> What thanks do you get for it all? They wither.

And, such is the mental process, I also recognize the contribution made by Arthur Guiterman's *On the Vanity of Earthly Greatness.* The theme of transitoriness and the final turn were unquestionably in my mind:

> The tusks that clashed in mighty brawls
> Of mastodons, are billiard balls.
>
> The sword of Charlemagne the Just
> Is ferric oxide, known as rust.
>
> The grizzly bear whose potent hug
> Was feared by all, is now a rug.
>
> Great Caesar's bust is on the shelf,
> And I don't feel so well myself!

Which makes me pretty derivative, I guess. But I belong to the critical school which insists that "we stand on the shoulders of the ancients." Not that Fishback, Hoffenstein, and Guiterman are exactly ancients, but their light verse affords the rest of us an elevated starting point.

Rich as is the field of young romance, even more material exists in the relationships of man and wife. Phyllis McGinley, in her *Husbands Are Difficult,* filled a book with delightful domestic pieces. Her Oliver Ames is a man worth knowing: a repository of all the weaknesses, eccentricities, and minor vices that a woman has ever deplored in her husband, and yet a man to be loved by all women who delight in mothering such a bundle of frailties. As a sample, there is this narrative of Oliver Ames' tour of the department stores with his indefatigable spouse:

THE FEMALE OF THE SPECIES IS HARDIER THAN THE MALE

> Oliver Ames is a stalwart man,
>   Whose strength is a gushing fountain.
> With a nonchalant smile he swims his mile
>   Or conquers the savage mountain.
> Girded for sport, he holds the fort
>   When rivals are round him dropping.
> But clear the deck
> For a Total Wreck
>   Whenever I take him shopping.
>
> Oliver is winded, Oliver's awry.
> He clutches at the counters and he plucks at his tie.
> On his overheated face
>   There's a weary sort of frown,
> And he's looking for a place
>   Where he can just sit down.
> And he mops at his brow
>   And he tugs at his cuff,
> And vows a mighty vow
>   That he's had about enough.

Now, a sturdy oak is Oliver Ames,
    While I am the ivy, twining.
I make no claims for my skill at games
    And I exercise best, reclining.
But when I'm out on a shopping bout
    Where the glittering price tags leer up,
Stouter and bolder,
It's always my shoulder
    That bolsters my frazzled dear up.

Saturday is young yet; I'm going like a breeze.
But Oliver is glassy-eyed and sagging at the knees.
We've only looked at draperies,
    We've only stormed the lifts
For silverware and naperies
    And half a dozen gifts;
We've only searched the basements
    For underwear and rugs
And curtains for our casements,
    And copper water jugs.

And still the time is ample
    For doing this and that.
I want to match a sample,
    I want to buy a hat.
I want to see the furniture that decks the Model House.
But Oliver is muttering the mutters of a spouse,
And his temper goes a-soaring
    While his metatarsals sink,
And he totters homeward, roaring
    For a pillow and a drink.

Oh, Delilah might have saved herself that legendary cropping
If she'd only taken Samson on a Saturday of shopping.

This also illustrates what amusing changes can be played
on a minor and already timeworn theme. Phyllis McGinley,

better than almost any other light verse writer, can develop a small idea into a swiftly-moving poem of many stanzas. Amusement grows and humor is enhanced with each new observation and unexpected turn. Inasmuch as light verse is usually paid for by the line, a study of her technique can be rewarding in the full sense of the word. While mentioning Phyllis McGinley, whose work I greatly admire, I might add that in recent years she seems to have moved from light verse to poetry of greater seriousness and significance. Light and serious, her poetic career reached a high point with the publication of *Times Three,* which won her the Pulitzer Prize.

The light verse writer should be married, if only to be able to observe married life at first hand. So also he should have children. For children, too, are a wonderful source of subjects. See, for example, Margaret Fishback's delightful book of prose and verse, *Who's a Mother?* There is a wealth of material in the infant, that small package of dampness and noise: waiting for it, first seeing it, naming it, deciding which parent it resembles, caring for it according to the book, and so on. A little mulling over the subject, accompanied apparently by a recollection of Gelett Burgess' *The Purple Cow,* once evoked this heartfelt reaction from me:

BABIES

I think whenever I see one
That I'd rather have been than still be one.

On this same subject, the birth of my son (named Geoffrey after Geoffrey Chaucer, my favorite poet) elicited these lines, published first in a magazine and then used to lead off a little book of mine called *For Partly Proud Parents*:

MINIATURE

My day-old son is plenty scrawny,
His mouth is wide with screams, or yawny,
His ears seem larger than he's needing,
His nose is flat, his chin's receding,
His skin is very very red,
He has no hair upon his head,
And yet I'm proud as proud can be
To hear you say he looks like me.

And then there are the humorous possibilities in the clash of theory and practice in the matter of child-raising, the race between wearing out and growing out of clothing, the constant struggle to keep the house tidy, or even intact, when youngsters come in from the out of doors and bring too much of it in with them. When he was small, my son provided me with a poem to match each vexation. He has been the begetter of many such pieces as this:

ON HIS MARKS

Junior's just a little tot,
    But handy with a pen.
He writes on walls, as soon as not,
    In living room and den.

Junior's very small, but still,
    With crayon and with paint,
He daubs the wall with right good will,
    Although we say he mayn't.

Junior scrawls, despite his age,
  With pencilings unstinted.
He can deface the title page
  Of any book that's printed.

Junior's destined to embark
  On some career quite steady.
I'm certain he will make his mark;
  In fact, he has already.

His younger sister, coming up right behind him, made it possible to glean the field for anything that might have been passed over at first harvesting. Adolescence, the period when growing really pains, is ghastly but fascinating. I have two excellent specimens at home, but I also observe the antics of neighborhood teen-agers in order to enrich my study of the species. May I suggest that an hour around the local high school should give anyone enough to write about for several days. Should it not, the pleasure of getting away from the place at the end of the hour would be worth the time spent. My observations at home and nearby provided me with material for many verses published in magazines and then scattered through my book, *Through Darkest Adolescence.*

The peccadilloes of human beings, regardless of age or sex, are innumerable. A new one will turn up every day, even if you do not look for it. Two will, if you do. In each of them there is the substance of a humorously satirical poem. The only restriction is that what is written about must be true of a great many people, and not merely of the writer himself or of some peculiar individual he alone has observed. The following, I believe, treats of an easily recognizable and quite general weakness:

Sing a Song of Silence

It pains me that at gatherings
When everyone around me sings
The old, familiar songs, I'm dumb
Or at the most I faintly hum.
Nor am I quiet out of choice,
Nor shamed because I lack the voice
With which to trill as do the birds—
I simply can't recall the words.

On the other hand, the following concerns a mannerism of which relatively few are guilty. And yet most people know at least one such offender.

Grip Gripe

Clasp my hand in fervent grip,
Shake it as you would a whip,
Pump it up and down with zest,
Make your friendship manifest,
But, I ask, don't make me stand
Minutes long with captive hand.
Shake it once more, high and low,
Then, I beg you, please let go.

To return to the generally applicable, are we not all familiar with man's desire to appear more generous than he is? This is manifested in many ways, for example:

Tip-off

The waitress doesn't need to wait
    Until she's closely eyed it:
The ten-cent tip's beneath the plate,
    The quarter tip's beside it.

I cite this partly because it can be handled quite as well from the opposite point of view, yielding two poems instead of one:

Take a Tip from Me

> I've given some thought to the whole wretched range
>   And believe that there are no extorters
> To rank with the waiters who bring back your change
>   In coins never smaller than quarters.

There are likewise all of those irritations that are not wholly man's fault, but the result of his unequal struggle with his man-made environment. Not monumental things, but things that annoy him plenty, such as how shoe laces always contrive to break in the most public spot; the way hotel walls have of being too thin to keep out the sleep-preventing noises from the next room, yet too thick to make it possible to overhear an interesting conversation; the carving knife that is too dull to cut anything except the end off one's finger; the shortage of paper towels in a public washroom, invariably discovered after one's hands and face are wet. The telephone is a good example of the sort of modern convenience whose inconveniences are grist for the light verse writer's mill. Two approaches to the subject are these:

For Whom the Bell Doesn't Toll

> Telephones are answered by
> Simple fellows such as I,
> Who, aroused from soundest slumbers,
> Skin their shins for misplaced numbers,

Or, with effort just as great,
Answer ringings, mostly late,
Then go trudging down the halls for
Those whom every single call's for.

PHONEY BUSINESS

My ringing phone, in dead of night,
  Rings on with such persistence,
I think the matter's urgent, quite,
  Or anyhow long distance.

It rings and rings while up I rise,
  And carries on its ringing
While, with the sleep still in my eyes,
  I down the stairs go springing.

It rings and rings and rings some more,
  And then, as is its habit,
It stops one single ring before
  I finally can grab it.

Man's physical environment, insofar as it baffles and
discomfits him, is always good for a piece of light verse.
Take the weather. Mark Twain might well have added to
his famous remark the observation that light verse writers
are always writing about it. There is its unpredictability,
with all due respect to the Weather Bureau; its perverse-
ness in time of picnic or garden party; the way the clouds
appear the instant you disrobe and get set for a sun bath;
the rain that descends from a recently cloudless sky to spot
the newly washed car. Closely related to this matter of
weather is the coming and going of the seasons, a constant
source of wonder—and of poems. *The New Yorker Book*

of Verse, to which I have already referred, is arranged by
the months of the year. It is noteworthy that a considerable
number of these poems, selected from the more than four
thousand that appeared during the first ten years of *The
New Yorker,* take their cue from the season. Thus there
is this February premonition of spring by E. B. White. Although a vignette of New York City, it is nonetheless familiar to anyone who knows the urban scene:

THE LADY IS COLD

Intimations at Fifty-Eighth Street

The fountain is dry at the Plaza,
    The sycamore trees go bare;
The ivy is sere and it has a
    Resigned and immutable air.

The lady is cold in the fountain,
    The sitter is cold on the ledge,
The Plaza is gaunt as a mountain,
    The air is a knife with an edge.

But what is this sniff and this twitter,
    And what is the pluck at my vest?
What gleam in the eye of the sitter?
    What lamb of a cloud in the west?

The earth is but held in solution,
    And March will release before long
The lady in brazen ablution,
    The trees and the fountain in song!

For my own part, I have written on each of the months,
going a little heavy on June, which I rather like, and Janu-
ary and February which annoy me most. It is chiefly the

irritating effect of the season on people, or the queer way people react to the season, that is the stuff of light verse. Here is an instance of making a mild complaint about the month that is otherwise probably the best of the year:

JUNE

June is the month to graduate
Or else to take oneself a mate;

And if one's getting neither bride
Nor sheepskin, one must still decide,

By dint of shopping near and far,
Just what to give to those who are.

An aspect of early spring that the more serious poets fail to hymn is this:

SINUS OF SPRING

Two-thirds winter, one-third spring,
March is almost sure to bring
One or two deceptive days
In the somewhat warmer phase.

Bright the sun and still the breeze,
Buds about to burst on trees,
Birds a-warble, kids at play.
Make the most of such a day.

So, to catch a breath of air,
Out one goes, and does not wear
Hat or coat and, overbold,
Beats one's chest—and catches cold!

The difference in attitude between the serious poet and the light verse writer is also indicated in the following

treatment of one of the manifestations of winter. In this
case the idea comes, indeed, from the very contrast of atti-
tudes:

So Red the Nose

When wintry winds blow strong and chill
On city street and rural hill,
The beauty-loving poet speaks
Of roses in fair ladies' cheeks.

But being of the honest kind,
I must admit, in truth, I find
The wintry blasts to bring the roses
Less oft to ladies' cheeks than noses.

Gardening is another rich field—to the light verse writer
if not to the gardener. There is that old devil weather again.
One might write a poem beginning:

Drought and flood,
Dust and mud . . .

and wonder whether there is any in-between. There are
bugs and weeds and the neighbor's dog, as well as tool bor-
rowers and people who insist on using the Latin names for
plants and flowers. There is, above all (or below all), the
good earth that is not always so good.

People, I have said, either in themselves or in relation to
other people or to their environment, are the most promising material for light verse. Almost as good, because also
living and lively, are birds and beasts and fish and insects.
But they must be written about from some unusual view-
point, usually somehow in comparison with people. Consider Ogden Nash in his poems about the turtle, the kitten,

the cow, and the panther; Hilaire Belloc on the hippopota-
mus and many another; Samuel Hoffenstein on the flea;
Mildred Weston on the squirrel. Each of these writers contrived to catch the humor that is in the living creatures that
pester, frighten, and sometimes befriend and cheer man—
in the zoo, in the jungle, and in the back yard. Ideas have
come to me from looking time and again at animals in
picture books and in real life, from the aardvark to the
zebra. Dogs and flies, probably because they are so ever-
present, have figured with special prominence in my verse.
As an example of writing about animals in conjunction
with human beings, I cite this:

SKIN GAME

The turtle, clam, and crab as well
Are covered with a sturdy shell,
While fish, excepting maybe whales,
Are shingled fore and aft with scales.

Though most, perhaps, have not the plating
Of armadillos, it's worth stating
That animals at least have hides
To give them fairly firm outsides.

And yet that upright mammal, man,
Must get along as best he can
With nothing but a little skin
To keep his precious insides in.

Ideas abound in the happenings of the day. Much light
verse is, after all, simply witty comment on current events,
passing fads, the social scene. Even World War II, which
had its lighter side as well as its tragic, and which had a

way of spotlighting the stupid and petty as well as the
heroic, gave me the ingredients of several hundred pieces,
including a book of verse on Army life and another volume
on the political aspects of the period. Rationing, blackouts,
alphabetical agencies, armchair military experts, ridiculous
pronouncements by the leaders of all the warring nations,
women in men's jobs, transportation difficulties. . . .
Those were halcyon days for satire. But the uneasy postwar
period, with its black market, its strikes, and its housing
shortage, proved almost as full of those irritations and inconsistencies on which light verse thrives. And the Space
Age of rockets and guided and misguided missiles and inter-
planetary travel is rich in ideas for playful and satirical
verse. Topical material is readily at hand in the newspaper,
in the newsreel, over the radio, and on TV. Of course it
won't wait. Unless the idea comes quickly and is worked up
into a poem without delay, someone else will have done the
job. It is like picking and shipping perishable fruit. However, new crops are always coming along. The next one
may not be quite as good, but you can be sure that there
will be a next one.

One further remark. Ideas come but rarely to one who
merely waits for an inspiration. They must be pursued,
wrestled with, and dragged home. Action on the writer's
part can take many forms, including close observation of
people and things, reading what others have written, and
thinking about likely subjects from first one point of view
and then another. It is encouraging to note that Berton
Braley, the dean of light verse writers since the death of
Arthur Guiterman, continues to turn up new ideas, even
after the publication of more than ten thousand poems. It

is not so encouraging, to some, to realize that he probably went out in diligent search of most of those ideas, and that he afterward sat very still in his chair for a long time converting them into poems. In short, ideas are everywhere, but there is work involved in getting them. And it is work that you can delegate to no one else.

CHAPTER FOUR

Meter Matters

GOOD light verse can be written without a detailed knowledge of versification. Although I hesitate to say so, too much technical knowledge may even be a handicap. By this I mean that the writer of light verse may labor mightily at his technique and bring forth a mouse of a poem, with nimbleness in its feet but not an idea in its head. Or he may be such a perfectionist that the labor never ends, and nothing comes forth. Obsession with form, particularly with inventing new metrical patterns, is the agonizing fault of many a beginner in the writing of poetry, whether serious or light. Despite my repeated assertion that metrical correctness is more necessary in light verse than in serious poetry, I must make certain here that the importance of form is not exaggerated in the mind of the reader. For I wholeheartedly agree with Louis Kronenberger, whose introduction to *An Anthology of Light Verse* I have already cited, when he says that "the technical side of the matter strikes me as vastly over-emphasized. Unless the versification is accompanied by substance and mood, the result is in the long run unhappily hollow. There are ever so many people today, for instance, who are flawless technicians—clever, ingenious, resourceful; yet, but little of their work proves really satisfying, and it is easy to see why. The stuff they write lacks temperament, character, charm; you merely admire it. It seldom makes you feel gayer for having read it, seldom gives you a glow, seldom is fun to reread." On the practical side, I have noticed that editors will buy a fresh and interesting idea, moderately well handled, in preference to an old or weak idea that is stated with better than average skill. Let the versification be of the best, but let it not be everything.

With this caution, I can safely say that much light verse is unsuccessful because it is either faulty or ineffective in expression. The meter may limp, the rhymes may be inexact, the thought may be obscure or undeveloped, the words may be poorly chosen, the conclusion may be lame. Poor technique can result from either carelessness or ignorance, neither of which is excusable. A certain amount of basic and easily acquired knowledge is absolutely necessary. One must be able to scan or count off the meters of a line of verse to make sure that it matches the length of another line. One must be able to tell when two words rhyme, and when they do not. One should be familiar with some of the time-tested verse and stanza forms which are ready-made molds for one's ideas and which make it unnecessary to invent new forms. One should also have an ear for the rhythm or music of verse, although in any but a rudimentary form this is more desirable than essential. As in any trade, certain tools are needed. Light verse requires fewer than most.

This is not the place for a bedrock beginning on the subject of versification. The reader will find all that he must know, and more, in Clement Wood's introduction to *The Complete Rhyming Dictionary,* a reference work which he will wish to keep at hand, anyhow, for its suggestion of rhymes. Or he can pursue the subject further with the always lucid and practical Clement Wood in his *Poet's Handbook.* My counsel, however, is to give less time to texts on the subject (including the book he is now reading) and more to a study of the light verse of his predecessors and competitors. Learning by example is, after all, the best method for the mastery of any skill, whether it be sculpture or skating, poetry or ping-pong. But some guidance might be helpful in indicating what to study and how to apply what is learned.

One reason why the light verse writer of our day need not be a master of intricate metrical forms is that the present-day reader does not care for them. Such elaborate patterns as the rondeau and the villanelle went out with the passing of gingerbread architecture, dust-catching furniture, and multi-layer petticoats. The Victorians suffocated light verse with pretty trappings, largely imported from the French. As we have become straightforward and functional about other things, so we have become more direct and less ornamental in our light verse. It is not likely that a magazine editor would give much attention today to such verbose versifying as Thomas Love Peacock's lines of a hundred years ago:

After careful meditation
And profound deliberation,
On the various pretty projects which have just been shown,
Not a scheme in agitation,
For the world's amelioration,
Has a grain of common sense in it, except my own.

Nor would one expect him to read many lines of a poem
with such a labored opening as C. S. Calverley's *Lines Suggested by the Fourteenth of February*:

Darkness succeeds to twilight:
Through lattice and through skylight,
The stars no doubt, if one looked out,
Might be observed to shine:
And sitting by the embers
I elevate my members
On a stray chair, and then and there
Commence a Valentine.

However skillful the versification, it does not suffice to hold
the attention while one waits for some semblance of an
idea to appear. Except for W. S. Gilbert, who sweeps the
critical reader away on the music of his verse—and who
proceeds very quickly to say pungent things—the old-time
jingle masters, full of prunes and prosody, are pretty tedious reading today. In my opinion, Phyllis McGinley can
match meters with any of them, and be far more entertaining doing it. One need not, and unless exceptionally
competent at it had better not, put one's faith in verse
fancywork. A little plain stitching is all that is called for.
   Of the many verse forms and stanzaic patterns that have
been employed in light verse, and were once thought prac-

tically required, only a handful are generally used today. The ballade, with its refrain and its envoi, still occasionally turns up, although with many modifications. Here is a good example of it from the accomplished pen of G. K. Chesterton:

A Ballade of Suicide

The gallows in my garden, people say,
Is new and neat and adequately tall.
I tie the noose on in a knowing way
As one that knots his necktie for a ball;
But just as all the neighbors—on the wall—
Are drawing a long breath to shout "Hurray!"
The strangest whim has seized me . . . After all
I think I will not hang myself to-day.

To-morrow is the time I get my pay—
My uncle's sword is hanging in the hall—
I see a little cloud all pink and grey—
Perhaps the Rector's mother will *not* call—
I fancy that I heard from Mr. Gall
That mushrooms could be cooked another way—
I never read the works of Juvenal—
I think I will not hang myself to-day.

The world will have another washing day;
The decadents decay; the pedants pall;
And H. G. Wells has found that children play,
And Bernard Shaw discovered that they squall;
Rationalists are growing rational—
And through thick woods one finds a stream astray,
So secret that the very sky seems small—
I think I will not hang myself to-day.

Envoi

Prince, I can hear the trumpet of Germinal,
The tumbrils toiling up the terrible way;
Even to-day your royal head may fall—
I think I will not hang myself to-day.

There is a certain satisfaction in the recognition of difficulty overcome, a pleasure in enjoying with the writer his success in meeting the stringent requirement he set for himself of writing his entire poem with but two rhyme sounds. But the idea might have been developed more naturally and inevitably without these artificial restrictions. In her justly famous *Resumé,* with its list of the various means of suicide, Dorothy Parker comes to the conclusion that "you might as well live" in just eight short lines. Not that her poem is any better than Chesterton's, but it is more in the modern manner of directness, conciseness, and simplicity of form. At any rate, if you are unable to cope with the ballade, take heart in the fact that you can get along very well without it.

Another form that light verse writers once thought they had to use occasionally, but that they have now all but given up, is the triolet. Artful and neat in its repetitions within a set pattern, it at least forces the writer to be brief. The trick is to get several different meanings out of the refrain line through changes in context or alterations of stress. An example from an earlier day is Austin Dobson's graceful poem, *A Kiss*:

Rose kissed me to-day.
    Will she kiss me to-morrow?
Let it be as it may,

Rose kissed me to-day.
But the pleasure gives way
  To a savour of sorrow;—
Rose kissed me to-day,—
  Will she kiss me to-morrow?

Nicely done, I admit. But to me, at least, a little of this sort of preciousness goes a long way.

Still on the negative side, there is one other form that has had its day. That is the limerick. Everyone likes to write limericks, and it seems that almost everyone can. Perhaps readers are only temporarily tired of them. The fact remains that the only writer of light verse who has had any marked success with them in recent years is Morris Bishop, who for a time published them rather regularly in *The New Yorker*. Even then, he was materially aided by R. Taylor's accompanying illustrations. Now Bishop too appears to have withdrawn from the publication of limericks. If he still writes them, he does so for his fortunate friends. After all, this is probably the best use for limericks, which are especially suited to oral transmission to a select and appreciative audience. Editors may smile at them, but they are almost sure to send them back.

So much for the forms that are outmoded or temporarily out of favor. What, then, is the light verse writer to use as the vehicle for his idea? It is my belief that couplets and quatrains are adequate for almost every occasion. Certainly they account for ninety-odd percent of the light verse being published today. They are usable in the short poem or in the long one. They are simple, easy to handle, relatively unrestrictive of the idea. They can be given additional interest and variety by internal and polysyllabic rhymes. They can be made more lilting through the use of anapestic feet. They are good general-service tools. But they should be kept sharp.

Here is an example of the couplet in the form most commonly found in light verse: rhyming lines of four iambic feet (iambic tetrameter). This happens also to be an instance of a poem consisting of a single couplet:

> Full fathom five thy father lies.
> I pushed him. I apologize.

The versification is simple, requiring the minimum of skill. Yet it is, at any rate, regular. There are neither too many nor too few syllables. The words are simple also, only three out of eleven having more than one syllable. And notice those three short sentences. It would be hard to write with more directness and economy. But if it seems unpoetic, let me point out that, of course, the first line is Shakespeare's. Only the second line is mine. What makes it funny, perhaps gruesomely so, is the sudden shift, the incongruity, after I took over. This couplet, which originally appeared in the *Saturday Review,* is included in my *Punctured Poems: Famous First and Infamous Second Lines,* a shamelessly irreverent book.

By skipping along with the anapest instead of walking with the iamb, one can write a couplet of the same type as to length of line but with more swing to it. An example is this:

Middle Man

The beginning, of course, is where movies begin at.
It's also the place that I rarely come in at.

Here the feet are uniformly anapestic, except for the beginning of the second line. By the use of "it is" instead of "it's," the couplet could have been made completely regular. Then why not do so? Because, unless the reader pauses solidly after "begin at," which he cannot be counted upon to do, three unaccented syllables are brought together in an awkward cluster. Furthermore, the informality of the contraction seems to me in keeping with the subject and mood. Light verse should be kept light by every means.

Couplets may be made up of shorter or longer lines than the four-foot line I have cited as the stock-in-trade of the light verse writer. Lines of five feet (pentameter) can sometimes be employed to good advantage, although they are generally more appropriate for serious poetry. Because they seem too heavy for most of my subjects, I usually pare them down from five feet to four, or break them into two lines. Lines of two and three feet, and for special effects one foot, can also be used. The following is an example of a couplet in anapestic lines of two feet each:

Let's Not Join the Ladies

After jokes told off-color,
Those *on* seem much duller.

I used short lines for this one because it seemed to me the humor, such as it is, depends on the quick follow-up of "off" by "on." So I wanted as few words as possible to come between the two. It would have been still better had I contrived to bring the sentence stress naturally upon the word "off," which I failed to do.

Normally the two lines of a couplet are of matching rhythm and equal length. But it is possible—though it should not be overdone—to gain novelty or surprise, or bring out the point it is desired to stress, by a violent break with the expected. That, in fact, is what this couplet relies upon:

WINTRY ANSWER

Where are the snows of yesteryear?
Here.

Thus far I have cited couplets that stand by themselves as complete poems. More often couplet is added to couplet until the thought is fully developed. Brevity being characteristic of light verse, four to twenty lines usually suffice, although hundreds may be needed to unfold a humorous narrative. Simple as the couplet is, one does not soon tire of it. In fact one is hardly conscious of the form being employed, if there is wit or humor in what is being said. Chaucer in his *Canterbury Tales* and Pope and Dryden in their satires found this true, and it is no less true today. It is only when the idea is too old or thin to stand on its own feet that it must be bolstered by an elaborate framework of verse. Even Ogden Nash, who is tagged as an individualist who flouts the conventions of prosody, writes an appreciable amount of his verse in carefully regular couplets. This is true, for example, of most of his delightful verses about animals and many of those wryly sentimental poems about his children and grandchildren. An instance of regular iambic tetrameter, rhyming in couplets, is his much-reprinted *Song of the Open Road*:

> I think that I shall never see
> A billboard lovely as a tree.
> Perhaps, unless the billboards fall,
> I'll never see a tree at all.

Although written quite without reference to the above, these lines of my own, in the same form, come to mind:

Another Leaf Shed by "Trees"

> Joyce Kilmer's lines may not be great
> But here and now I rise to state
> I'd rather far have written "Trees"
> Than all its thousand parodies.

In a poem in couplet form, the lines may be either end-stopped (an end of the thought or a natural pause coinciding with the end of the line) or run-on (the thought continuing without a marked break at the end of the line). Too much of the end-stopped type of line may cause stiffness and monotony; too much of the run-on type may throw the reader off the track. What the writer is after is to make his poem read naturally. It should seem to roll along without effort. A reasonably good example of what I have in mind, a mixture of end-stopped and run-on lines, is the following:

The Fly

> The fly, though not invited in,
> Comes anyhow, and brings his kin.
> He zooms about the place at first,

Full of exploratory thirst,
And like an Alpine climber crawls
Atop the pictures on the walls,
Or, with an utter lack of feeling,
Walks upside down across the ceiling.
He soars and swoops and often lands
Upon your forehead, nose, or hands.
He kibitzes when you're at table
And samples all the food he's able,
And though he leaves whenever shooed,
He comes again when in the mood.
Upon a sunny ledge where it's
As balmy as a beach, he sits
And preens his wings and rubs his face
And acts as if he owns the place,
Till, having reached his span allotted,
The end comes quickly: he is swatted.

The punctuation is worth noting here. In order to guide
the reader, especially when run-on lines are prevalent, it is
important that the proper signposts be employed. Before
leaving this poem, I should also like to call attention to
the fourth line, "Full of exploratory thirst." Remembering
Pope's "ten low words oft creep in one dull line," I am
always glad to work in an apt polysyllable. Nor can I forget
such a triumph as Herrick scored with the "liquefaction"
of Julia's clothes. But this is a minor matter, and something
better left alone than overdone. Just work for naturalness,
fluency, and grace.

One further remark about poems written in the couplet
form. They need not be set down without break. It is sometimes desirable to cut them up into stanzas of equal length,
say four or six lines each, or to group them into stanzas of
varying size, like prose paragraphs, to indicate shifts in

thought. Occasionally it may be found effective to space between couplets and thus emphasize the unity of each. I did this in the following, which appeared in *The Saturday Evening Post*:

STRANGE WOMEN ARE STRANGE INDEED

They make their lips all red and kissable,
But kissing them is not permissible.

They diet till they're svelte and curvy,
But if you ogle, think you're nervy.

They put on perfume meant to trap you,
But if you sniff too close, they slap you.

They slink and sway in way improper,
But if you follow, call a copper.

They first attract and then repel you.
You fall for them, and then they fell you.

Like correct punctuation, this is a means of guiding the reader to the desired thought and emphasis. If it gives the poem a more attractive appearance on the printed page, it may also invite reading.

I have indicated that you can do just about anything you want to in the field of light verse with the simple couplet form alone. To be really well equipped, add the quatrain —four lines grouped in one or another of several combinations of rhythm, line length, and rhyme. A few of these combinations are as follows:

1. Lines of four and three feet alternately, the first and

third and second and fourth lines rhyming (*abab*). With iambic meter and single-syllable rhymes—in other words very simply and regularly—it goes like this:

COMPARATIVELY SPEAKING

The faithful dog will roam at night,
  The strongest iron will rust,
The cooing dove is not so bright,
  The good earth's also dust.

Thorns mar the sweetly scented rose,
  A stinger has the bee,
So with this little thought I close:
  Don't ask too much of me!

Indention of the rhyming lines, as here, is usual practice. It helps the reader match the rhymes and see what the writer is up to. It will also be noticed that the words in the second line of the second stanza are not in their conventional order. "A stinger has the bee," it reads, instead of "the bee has a stinger." This is a privilege of the poet, exercised for the sake of rhythm, rhyme, and emphasis. Such inversions should, however, be resorted to infrequently. The ability to follow the normal word order, despite the restrictions of the verse pattern, is one of the marks of the professional. A poem can be seriously marred by one or two lines in which the words are grotesquely out of their regular order, obviously because the poet lacked the skill or the patience to fit them naturally into his system of meter and rhyme.

2. Lines of the same length, with alternating rhymes. While the lines may be as short as two or three feet, or

even one foot, the four-foot line is most usual in light verse. Here is a poem made up of quatrains (*abab*) in which all the lines consist of three feet:

So My Wife Tells Me

A husband takes insisting,
    A husband's rather slow.
It may require some twisting
    Of arms before he'll go

To picnic or to party,
    To mountains or to shore,
To something gay and hearty,
    Or something tame next door.

In fact the only prodding
    As great as this is when
You try (it's late, you're nodding)
    To get him home again.

This was one of four poems of mine in the same issue of *Better Homes and Gardens,* establishing a record which I have never equalled. Notice that, while the meter is still iambic, a fillip is given by the use of double rhymes in the first and third line of each stanza (*insisting-twisting, party-hearty, prodding-nodding*).

An instance of the more usual quatrain with lines of four feet throughout is this:

Distant Views

Two sayings that I've been inclined
    In puzzlement ofttimes to ponder
Are "Out of sight is out of mind"
    And "Absence makes the heart grow fonder."

They're opposite as day and night,
   The very height of contradiction,
No more alike than black and white,
   Or large and small, or fact and fiction.

To reconcile them, though, I've quit;
   It's not a thing I'm growing gray from,
For I have found, at last, that it
   Depends on whom you are away from.

I know that the poem would have been sprightlier with three instead of four feet in the second and fourth lines of each stanza. But the length of the quotation, "Absence makes the heart grow fonder," dictated the pattern, which then had to be followed through consistently. Again the meter is strictly iambic, although the two-syllable rhymes, this time in the second and fourth lines (*ponder-fonder,* etc.) have an enlivening effect. In the next-to-last line of the poem, the phrase "at last" was admittedly thrown in to fill out the line. Since it is not too obvious and does add a little to the meaning, it can perhaps be forgiven. Ordinarily, when such a tag plainly serves no purpose but to make the meter come out right, it should be avoided, if at all possible, through revision either of the line or of the entire stanza.

3. Quatrains in which the lines are of the same or alternately different length and the first and fourth and second and third lines rhyme (*abba*). Because the first and last rhyme-sounds are so far apart, this is a form that is not very popular, especially in light verse. An example of it in serious poetry, for which it is somewhat better suited, is Tennyson's *In Memoriam,* which opens with this quatrain:

> I held it truth, with him who sings
>   To one clear harp in divers tones,
>   That men may rise on stepping-stones
> Of their dead selves to higher things.

Many are the combinations and permutations of the quatrain. To lend emphasis to an unexpected ending one may, as Robert Burns did with such good effect a century and a half ago, drop a foot out of the last line. To illustrate this, I cite this quatrain of my own:

ENDS AND MEANS

> To educate a boy's an art
>   That takes parental care.
> We know just how to make him smart—
>   And also where!

In the usual quatrain, the fourth line, matching in length the second, would have read "And also we know where." Yet it would manifestly have been less effective. One may also, as in the following, add zest and speed up the movement by using anapestic feet and internal rhymes (*aisle-smile, rare-pair*):

TO HAVE AND TOO OLD

> The bride, white of hair, is stooped over her cane,
>   Her footsteps, uncertain, need guiding,
> While down the church aisle, with a wan, toothless smile,
>   The groom in a wheel chair comes riding.

> And who is this elderly couple, thus wed?
>   You'll find, when you've closely explored it,
> That here is that rare, most conservative pair,
>   Who waited till they could afford it.

It is also possible to combine the quatrain and the couplet to get various effects of novelty and emphasis. W. E. Farbstein, a contemporary light verse writer, has had considerable success with his use of the quatrain followed immediately by a couplet. In the couplet he sums up, makes an odd comparison, comes out with an unexpected conclusion, or otherwise ends his poem divertingly. I confess to having borrowed his technique in a number of pieces. One of these is the following:

YOU TAKE THE HIGH DIVE

Admiringly I leave the swan,
　　The jackknife, and the gainer
To lifeguard and to amazon
　　While I do something plainer,
Such as by accident to fall in
Or else, when no one's looking, crawl in.

Although almost any idea can be adequately treated with the couplet or quatrain, I suggest another easy form that is worth adding to your tool kit—or, if the figure of the poet at play is sustained, to your bag of clubs. This is the six-line stanza consisting of a couplet, then another longer or shorter line, then another couplet, and finally a line that matches in length, and rhymes with, the third line (*aabccb*). Here is one example of it:

THE CRITIC

The critic is a fellow who
Can read an author's opus through
　　And highly praise or mercilessly pan it,

Discovering, as on he reads,
The evidence he feels he needs
   To back the views he had when he began it.

And here is another, with the third and sixth lines shorter,
rather than longer:

Cup That Doesn't Cheer

I wish, as drowsily I hear
The words still drumming on my ear
   While evening passes,
That after-dinner speeches, same
As after-dinner coffee, came
   In demitasses.

Finally, I give you an instance of sheer invention to
meet a need. It is the sort of thing which, I hope I have
made clear, is justified only on rare occasions. If used frequently, it would become mannered and tiresome.

Hotel Lobby

The people who merely meet there
And rest their backs and feet there
And fill up every seat there
   One cannot tell
   So very well
From those who sleep and eat there.

By way of a personal note on the inception, composition,
and publication of the above, I might add that the idea
came to me while I was resting my back and feet in the
lobby of a hotel in Atlanta, Georgia. It was wartime, and
the place was crowded. Once having captured a seat, I had
a guilty sense of depriving a paying guest of it. But I felt

secure in the thought that, just as I was unable to distinguish the inhabitant from the interloper, neither could anyone else. This seemed to me a good idea for a piece of light verse, and I worked out the lines (undoubtedly looking very busy to the other idlers) while I sat in the lobby. Later, in the belief that human nature in an Atlanta hotel lobby is much the same as human nature in the grander foyers of Manhattan, I dispatched the poem to *The New Yorker,* which published it.

To sum up, it is necessary to know and have facility with only a few simple verse forms, chiefly the couplet and the quatrain. Time and energy can more profitably be devoted to searching for ideas and polishing their presentation in these much-used forms than in contriving something of your own. As my main point might be expressed in verse:

> Now, in closing, one last touch—
> This I mean by all my chatter:
> Meter matters, matters much,
> But it matters less than matter.

CHAPTER FIVE

Rhyme Does Pay

IT is a matter of taste, but I cling to the old-fashioned belief that rhyme usually adds interest and beauty to poetry of "higher truth and higher seriousness," in Matthew Arnold's phrase, as well as to light verse. To give up both rhyme and meter (except for a vaguely recurrent rhythm), as many free verse moderns do, is to deny the reader one of the pleasures he expects from poetry and to avoid, for himself, a discipline that can sharpen the poet's art. I am inclined to agree with Robert Frost, who compared the writing of free verse to playing tennis with the net down.

But the foregoing is perhaps extraneous, for the light verse writer is not likely to employ either free or blank verse forms. It should be apparent that rhyme, no less than meter, is a prime requisite of light verse, whether or not it is desirable in serious poetry. This is not to say that rhyme-less light verse cannot be written and published, but ex-

66

amples of it take a deal of looking for. One instance I can think of, if it was intended to be a poem and not merely a prose epigram broken into lines that give the appearance of verse, is Don Marquis's *prohibition:*

> prohibition makes you
> want to cry
> into your beer and
> denies you the beer
> to cry into

Even here, I should have liked it better if Archy had been able to work the capital levers on his typewriter, and if he had owned a rhyming dictionary.

Light verse requires not only rhymes, but exact ones. Here again the serious poets have, or at least take, more latitude. They can get away with eye rhymes (words that look to the eye as if they rhyme but which actually do not rhyme in sound), like *love-prove, war-star, earth-hearth.* They can use, and some of them even affect, approximate rhymes. Assonance (repetition of final vowel sounds, followed by different consonantal sounds, such as *mate-shape, head-neck*) and consonance (repetition of final consonantal sounds, preceded by different vowel sounds, such as *lost-ghost, gather-weather*) are being increasingly used in serious poetry to enlarge the possibilities of rhyme. But light verse, unsupported by high thought and strong emotion, cannot afford such approximate and partial rhyming. The average reader wants and expects, in light verse, rhymes that are accurate and complete.

To be avoided are "identities." These (like *ball-bawl, piece-peace*) are not true rhymes, because, while there is the desired repetition of vowel sound, there is no variety in the preceding consonantal sound. Rhymes depending on mispronunciation (*purr-orchestra,* which might rhyme when spoken by a native of Maine; *burden-wording,* which requires the dropping of the "g") should likewise be avoided if at all possible.

Just how fastidious editors can be in this matter of rhyming is illustrated by a near-rejection I once experienced. A poem was returned by *The Saturday Evening Post* for revision because, taking advantage of a colloquial pronunciation permitted by Webster, I had rhymed "route" with "about." The editor rightly felt that some readers would have misread my lines as they were, and possibly have been thrown off the track of thought. And in a short piece of humorous verse you must keep the reader with you literally every foot of the way. In my revision of the two lines in question, I eliminated "route" entirely and produced a *doubt-about* rhyme that no one could question. The revised poem was purchased, to my relief and gratification. The incident taught me to be more careful with my rhymes and to consider them always from the point of view of the reader.

Harder to detect are rhymes that have become hackneyed and obvious by being overworked. Instances from the song-writers are *love-above, June-moon,* and *trees-breeze.* The most shopworn I can think of in beginners' light verse are *poet-know it* and *college-knowledge. Trouble-double, remember-December,* and *money-funny* are among the many that have long since lost their luster but that one is sometimes compelled to use. In the fight against obviousness, one little trick I employ is to select rhyming words, when possible, that *look* different, although they match precisely in sound. Thus, if the opportunity were to present itself, I would pair *bite-height* instead of *bite-white,* or *some-thumb* instead of *some-come.* When using polysyllabic rhymes, I like to avoid words of the same number of syllables. My reason is that such words are too pat and too likely to be anticipated by the reader, with whom, after all, I am playing a sort of game. So I would prefer *tinkle-periwinkle* to *tinkle-wrinkle,* and *function-compunction* to *function-junction.* But I call upon such a device only when everything else is equal. Should I permit it to interfere in the slightest degree with either the idea that is being expressed or the apparently unstudied and natural way of expressing it, I would be tripping myself with my own rope. In my eagerness to keep from being trite I do, all too frequently, take a fall.

Incorrect, hackneyed, self-conscious rhymes can be damaging, but clever, unanticipated, humorous rhymes, worked naturally into the sequence of thought, can do wonders for a piece of light verse. Clement Wood, in his *Complete Rhyming Dictionary,* asserts that rhyming cleverness in light verse "is a crown."

The unusual and the humorous are most likely to be achieved with polysyllabic rhymes—rhymes of two or three syllables. While the serious poet must use these sparingly, the light verse writer can work them in almost as much as he likes. He has ample precedent. The Cavalier poets of the seventeenth century were singularly adept at this kind of rhyming. Herrick, for instance, matches in a single short poem *lend thee, attend thee,* and *befriend thee,* as well as *bite thee, affright thee,* and *mislight thee,* while Suckling rhymes *lover-mover* and *sinner-winner.* Burns, with both pure English and a Scottish dialect to draw upon, could rhyme *glitter-butter, barrels-morals, heathen-faith in,* and even *at us-potatoes.* The latter makes one wonder whether he said *ate oze* for *at us* or *potattus* for *potatoes.* Perhaps he was amusing himself with pronunciation as well as rhyme. Byron was another resourceful rhymester. In his *Beppo,* he rhymes *fantastical-gymnastical-ecclesiastical* (a three-syllable rhyme), *balcony* (which he apparently pronounced *balcō'ny*)-*Giorgione,* and *stanzas-dance as-France has.* In *Don Juan,* his rhyme *of ineffectual-henpecked you all* is deservedly famous. Few have been able to combine fresh, amusing, seemingly inevitable rhymes with dancing rhythm so well as W. S. Gilbert, whose lines about that latter-day Falstaff, the Duke of Plaza-Toro, cry out for quoting, if not singing:

> In enterprise of martial kind,
>   When there was any fighting,
> He led his regiment from behind
>   (He found it less exciting).
> But when away his regiment ran,
>   His place was at the fore, O—
>   That celebrated,
>   Cultivated,
>   Underrated
>   Nobleman,
>   The Duke of Plaza-Toro! . . .

> When, to evade Destruction's hand,
>   To hide they all proceeded,
> No soldier in that gallant band
>   Hid half so well as he did.
> He lay concealed throughout the war,
>   And so preserved his gore, O!

> That unaffected,
> Undetected,
> Well connected
> Warrior,
> The Duke of Plaza-Toro!

Double and triple rhymes are sometimes managed by matching polysyllabic words. Almost as often, two or more short words are rhymed with a single longer one, or two words with two words. Phyllis McGinley is much given to unexpected combinations of words that rhyme with single words or other combinations of words, for example: *baton-hat on, assail her-Lord & Taylor, hook up-look up, circuit-work it, viewpoint-new point,* and *pastime-last time.* She is usually careful to use the single word or the ordinary combination of words first, and then in the rhyming line to come up with something that seems made to order but that would probably not have occurred to you. To do it the other way around would, she well knows, be to give the reader the answer before the question, and to let him down rather than lift him up. It is a little point worth noting.

Phyllis McGinley, by the way, now and then doctors up a spelling, or italicizes to indicate an unorthodox accent, in order to accomplish her rhyme. Examples are her *sand-wiches-bandwiches, lotused-notuced,* and *syllabelles are-Orson Welles' are.* But she resorts to this sort of thing only rarely. Generally she is ingenious enough to get herself out of an apparent impasse by fair means. After all, there are few words for which no rhyme can be found, if the poet is patient and resourceful. The late William Rose Benét rediscovered the truth of this when he dropped the remark, in his column in *The Saturday Review of Litera-*

ture, that it seemed impossible to rhyme the word "erysip-elas." Scores of his readers promptly proved to him that it could be done. And I know a college professor whose favorite indoor game is to ask his guests to tell him a rhyme for some such word as "window." When they give up, he has one ready, and beams with pleasure over this demonstration of his superiority. (If you are having trouble, try "thin doe.")

As there is an exception to every rule, so there is to this one against the distortion of the spelling and pronunciation of words in order to make them rhyme. This exception is, by name, Ogden Nash. Oddity of rhyme, including the brashest coinages, is perfectly in keeping with his intentionally irregular meter and his madcap thought. Such rhymes as *unreliable-Biable, populace-metropulace, panther-anther, porterhouse-slorterhouse,* and of course *rhinoceros-prepoceros* are not only appropriate in Ogden Nash's verses but eagerly expected by the reader, who would be disappointed not to encounter them. Ogden Nash is an outstanding example of the poet at play, and his rhyming is a key part of the game. When he discusses the literary taste of children and states that

Innocent infants have no use for fables about rabbits or donkeys or tortoises or porpoises,

the reader is curious not only about what he is going to say next, but how he is going to contrive a rhyme. He comes up to expectations in both respects:

What they want is something with plenty of well-mutilated corpoises.

But even he does not overdo these manufactured rhymes. Most of the time he manages to rhyme troublesome words without alteration of either spelling or pronunciation. Such rhymes as these indicate his resourcefulness: *human-albumen, chamois-mammy, scissored-lizard, chapter-apter, dairy can-American, sunset-Sigrid Undset, used to-introduced to, sail for it-jail for it.* Comparable pairings are everywhere in his verses. Those erratic long lines of his, which make the reader wait in suspense for the rhyme that is at the end, further heighten the humor. However, Ogden Nash has made these techniques so much his own that he may be considered to have copyrighted them. He is to be enjoyed and admired, but not copied. One is not likely to achieve his special blend of freewheeling thought and uninhibited expression—which takes more talent and craftsmanship than at first appears. And what if one should? It would almost certainly mean being branded an imitator.

An unusual rhyme can of itself make a poem. Indeed, it can almost be the whole of the poem. A case in point is this little piece:

Photo Finish

With girls renowned
   For having glamour a
Lot depends
   Upon the camera.

Actually a couplet, I broke it into four lines in order to slow up the reader and make the rhyme, which is the main thing, stand out. Another short poem in which the rhyme is important, if not quite everything, is the following:

ON SEEING AN X-RAY PICTURE OF MYSELF

Although I've really never been
Entranced with my exterior,
I must admit I'm glad for skin,
My inside's so much eerier.

Both of the above poems use three-syllable rhymes. One trouble with this type of rhyme is that it may be stumbled over at first reading, and a first reading may be all it will get. Two-syllable rhymes, though less likely to be unusual, are more easily read. *Door,* which follows, is an example of a poem containing (in the second and fourth lines of each stanza) two-syllable rhymes. They are, I believe, of considerable help in gaining whatever humor the piece possesses.

It takes long years to grow the wood
For oak or even pine one,
It takes some skill, I've understood,
To measure and design one.

It takes a painter just to paint,
A carpenter to hang one,
And yet—and this is my complaint—
The merest child can bang one.

The next is a quatrain with two-syllable rhymes throughout:

Lines Long Before Christmas

To this, ere the snowflakes come swirling,
    I know that I'm sure to be fated:
The gifts that I give will be sterling,
    While those I receive will be plated.

Again, it was the rhyming that brought the verse up to the level of amusement that meant a sale instead of a rejection.

I have said that the three-syllable rhyme is a little hard to read. This obstacle can usually be overcome if a firm pattern is established at the beginning of a poem. Then the reader knows what to expect, and moves along without difficulty. I can think of one occasion when a rhyme (in this case *highnesses-sinuses*) gave me an idea and also caused me deliberately to develop the thought with three-syllable rhymes throughout. Any variation would have been distracting. My problem was to hold to the three-syllable rhyme from start to already-written finish, and to reject any one- or two-syllable rhymes that might come to mind along the way. What I might have left as a mere couplet,

> Even royal highnesses
> Have trouble with their sinuses,

I expanded into a poem of fair length. And I think the humor was increased both by dwelling longer on the idea and by piling one three-syllable rhyme upon another. This is the way it came out:

THE EXTREMELY COMMON COLD

Of all the ills iniquitous
The cold is most ubiquitous.
Throughout the whole community
No one has much immunity.
It comes to every national,
To sane and to irrational,
To debtor and to creditor,
Illiterate and editor,
To wicked and to pious folk,
To open-mind and bias folk,
To high as well as low degree,
To college grad and no degree.
And though you sneeze and cough a lot,
It helps, though not an awful lot,
To know that there's no preference
Regarding colds, nor deference,
And even royal highnesses
Have trouble with their sinuses.

I have a sneaking feeling that my *awful lot-cough a lot*
rhyme owes, however slightly, to a chant that has lingered
in my head since boyhood:

> It wasn't the cough
> That carried him off;
> It was the coffin
> They carried him off in.

A word should be said of that useful device, internal
rhyme. This is the rhyme of a word in the middle of the
line with that at the end of the line. By suddenly bringing
rhyming sounds close together, you may gain additional
lift. In the following, the words involved in internal rhyme
are italicized:

Shooting Irony

The huntsman pays his hunting fee,
Refurbishes his gear up,
And with his *gun* to have some *fun*
Goes looking him a deer up.

He has his license, has his gun,
He has his huntsman's zoot hat,
He has, *indeed,* all one could *need,*
Except a deer to shoot at.

Although I shall discuss endings in more detail in the next chapter, it is appropriate to state here that a smart, unanticipated rhyme can be put to excellent use to cap off a poem. It seems to say, "So there!" It heightens the humor at the very point where it should be highest, and it gives a sense of finality when you want the reader to know that you are through. I like to save a good rhyme, often a two- or three-syllable one, for the end. It is like eating last the nut on the cookie. While a strong rhyme is of particular help as the terminus of a poem of some length, the following illustrates what it will do even for a quatrain:

Ends of Means

The more I earn, the more I spend.
There's always nothing, in the end.
From this my present fear and doubt come:
I can't control my income's outcome.

Consider the difference if the *doubt come-outcome* rhyme had fallen in the first two lines and the commonplace *spend-end* rhyme had come in the last two. Despite the fact that it is not the only two-syllable rhyme, as was true in *Ends of Means,* the one at the close of the following piece seems to me also to add to the fun of the ending:

FABLE

The sluggard was counseled to go to the ant,
   In hope that the latter's example
Would cause him his indolent ways to recant
   And give up his leisure so ample.

The sluggard, congenial, dropped in on the ant,
   Who, hard at his work, ever kept on,
Until by the sluggard (who still is extant)
   He was, most regrettably, stepped on.

One question that is certain to arise about rhymes is how to find them. Some rhymes will spring to mind at once, without effort or coaxing. These, quite possibly, will be the best ones. Coming into being naturally, they will appear natural to the reader. And naturalness, or inevitability, is much to be desired. Other rhymes will have to be discovered by the good old method of running through the alphabet. I find myself doing this over and over again. Thus if I should want a rhyme for *quicker,* I would think through the alphabet and find myself *bicker, kicker, dicker, flicker, liquor, nicker, picker, sicker, sticker, ticker,* and *wicker.* Should none of these happen to suit, I would then turn to my rhyming dictionary to see whether I had missed any possibilities. There I would find, among others that I had overlooked, *clicker, knicker, thicker, tricker,* and *vicar.* If I still did not have what I needed, I might try putting two words together, such as *trick her* or *sick cur.* In the end I might either be successful in my search or, failing, be forced to abandon *quicker*, and perhaps all or part of my initial idea with it, for lack of a suitable rhyme. It would be better to admit defeat, however unwillingly, than to force a rhyme that was noticeably inexact or too obvious a makeshift.

Rhyming becomes ever easier with practice. It is a matter of hunting and testing and choosing. In time, the process becomes habitual. But it should never become haphazard or careless. For correct, fresh rhymes are an integral part of light verse. Really good ones are, indeed, its crown.

CHAPTER SIX

Ends and Means

A PIECE of light verse can be made or unmade by its last stanza, last line, or even last word. It may open weakly and proceed in undistinguished fashion through the middle, but it *must* end strongly. Unlike the novel and the drama, which frequently attain their climax some distance from the final chapter or scene, light verse almost invariably reaches its end and rises to its climax simultaneously. Unlike serious poetry, which may spread its power fairly evenly over the whole, light verse usually concentrates its force at the close. The preceding lines are the fuse that burns, however merrily, up to the explosive charge that is cached alongside the final period. There's a divinity that shapes our ends. If there is any inspiration in writing light verse, this is the place for it.

It is hard to explain what makes a good ending for a humorous or amusing poem. Obviously, it should be the most intensive part of the humor, the height of the amusement. If the reader is to laugh or smile at any place in his reading, it will be here, at the end. As in a joke, it is here that the point will be made or will not. The reader will be satisfied and pleased with having been led this far, because of what he has received for his pains, or he will be dissatisfied and displeased because what is disclosed fails to come up to what he had expected. Ideally, he will be so happy about it that he will read the poem aloud to someone else, and note with vicarious pleasure the impact of the ending. An effective ending will very likely have an element of surprise in it. There will be newness either in the thought or in the manner of expressing it. Also, like any literary climax, it will be the accumulation or product of what has gone before. It will be led up to, and not merely tacked on. The reader will be ready and waiting, and will be forced to wait just the right length of time. Finally, he will be rewarded up to, or beyond, his expectations.

Sometimes, especially in a very short poem, the ending is little more than the completion of a statement. Because the beginning, middle, and end are essentially one, the ending has no special quality. An example is this quatrain:

CONSIDER THE SOURCE

One thing that is sure to annoy you
As almost no other thing does
Is being described as a has-been
By someone who never was.

But even here there is a pairing off of opposites, in the last two lines, the intention being to entertain the reader with a neat, if only mildly amusing, bit of wordplay. Cer-

tainly the point is made in the last lines. The first two
merely lead up to it. To prove that this is true, notice
what happens when the lines are turned around:

> Being described as a has-been
>   By someone who never was
> Is one thing that's sure to annoy you
>   As almost no other thing does.

The idea is unchanged, but the presentation of it is flat.
The two lines that follow the main point serve to dilute
it and make it a commonplace statement of fact. Remove
the rhyme, by a slight change in the word order, and you
have the thought in prose: "Being described as a has-been
by someone who never was is one thing that is sure to
annoy you as does almost no other thing." It is no longer
even a very good epigram. And yet with the employment
of rhythm and rhyme, with a bit of wordplay, and—most
important—with the climax at the end where it belongs,
it is a fairly respectable bit of light verse.

In most instances, however, the ending is likely to be
more conspicuous, although still well knit into the poem.
Usually there is an element of surprise, or an unforesee-
able twist in the thought. The reader is led toward a goal
that he thinks he discerns, and then suddenly, at the very
end, is headed off in another direction, to something he
had not suspected. Or, to put it another way, the writer
chats pleasantly with him while they walk along a harm-
less-looking, well-lit hallway, and then adroitly steps aside
while the reader falls through the carefully concealed trap-
door. This is approximately what happens here:

LEASE MAJESTY

I scheme and plot to circumvent
The landlord who declines to rent
Because I have a little son,
A precious child, my only one.

I ask him if he once were not
A child himself, a playful tot,
A merry youth, a bit carousing,
Who needed, just as mine, some housing,

Or if he ever gave a thought
To how the world would wag, and what
Would be, in time, the net result
If everyone were an adult.

But naught I do will turn the trick.
The landlord's shrewd. His hide is thick.
I cannot scare, I cannot shame him.
(And what is more, I don't much blame him.)

Also this, which down to the last line seems to be a lyrical
effusion of the pipes-of-Pan school:

WISHFUL THINKING

If I had the wings of a bird of the air
    And the fins of a fish of the sea,
I could travel with speed and abandon all care,
    I could ramble the wide world free.

The wings of a bird and the fins of a fish,
    As well as the legs of a deer—
I could fly, I could swim, I could run as I wish,
    But I'd certainly look mighty queer.

The above is also fairly typical of the way the light verse writer pricks the ballooning serious emotion. The more abrupt the drop and the harder the fall, the more fun it is. In *Wishful Thinking*, it happens that the joke is not only on the reader but on the poet, who works himself up a fancy daydream and then suddenly awakens to cold reality. There is incongruity here also—a contrast between the fanciful and the practical—and recognition of the incongruous is one of the fundamentals of humor, in light verse or wherever it is found. The following is an example of a less violent concluding twist:

LINES OF A LATE VACATIONER

I hate to come late to the beach
  When others are already tanned
While I look so white that it gives me a fright.
  (I'm just brown on the back of my hand.)

I hate to come late to the beach
  And look like a pale hothouse lily.
Amongst all the tawny, the bronzed and the brawny,
  I feel somewhat naked and silly.

I hate to come late to the beach
  And feel like a wan second-rater,
Except that the brown soon must go back to town,
  While I stay to awe the still later.

The last stanza, it will be noted, might have stood by itself as the entire poem. But the reiteration of the opening idea is important. The purpose of the first ten lines is to dwell on the thought until the reader is thoroughly convinced of the regrettability of being a late comer at the beach. Then the unlooked-for exception pops up at the end.

In this connection, it is frequently effective to open a poem with the statement of a well-known axiom or expression. Since it is already accepted as true by the reader, there is no need to groove his thought in a certain direction. No such repetition for this purpose, as in *Lines of a Late Vacationer,* is called for. All that remains, after statement of the truism, is to develop it in some perverse way. The following is a twist on the old saw, "You can't keep a good man down":

PERSONNEL OPINION

You can't keep a good man down.
   The times I have heard this are myriad.
In fact, as employers know,
   You can't keep a good man, period.

The next is an example of discovering a time-honored saying to be incomplete and one-sided:

OBJECT LESSON

We all have very often heard
About the clever early bird
Who gets the worm and who is thus
Supposed to demonstrate to us
The sure advantages to man
Of being always in the van.
The story, though, however old,
Is never quite completely told,
For of the eager early worm
Who simply cannot wait to squirm
And so is up to greet the bird,
We never hear a single word.

An expression that has been used at one time or another by almost everyone is "I can read you like a book." It can be given the following treatment, which involves addition to, and new direction of, the original thought:

READING MATTER

People say, with piercing look,
"I can read you like a book."

Whereupon I bow my head
And submit to being read,

Hoping, with a hope quite grim,
They're the kind who merely skim.

One of the best opportunities for a neat, pointed ending is in the use of a pun. The following quatrains rely upon wordplay of one kind or another.

SO FAR, SO BAD

When I say your new hat is becoming, my dear,
I mean it, although I look glum.
Becoming, I swear, is the word, for I fear
It hasn't, as yet, quite become.

OATHS OF OFFICE

He'll find, should he win
The office sought, that
One day he's sworn in,
The next, he's sworn at.

POUND FOOLISH

This is fate, as sure as sin:
One grows fat, the other thin.
Man and wife move all their days
Toward a parting of the weighs.

Sometimes the wordplay can be embarked upon early in the poem and carried through to the conclusion. This is done in the poem that follows, which is further pointed up by the short final line:

OF ALL THE NERVE

It's very easy to observe
That those who have a lot of nerve
   Have also got
A way of breaking through reserves
And someday getting on the nerves
   Of those who've not.

Or the wordplay may be slowly led up to and not appear until the closing sentence or phrase:

WELL NAMED

I picnic on the sandy beach,
   The breeze is briskly blowing,
And, as for sandwiches I reach,
   A crowd keeps to-and-froing.

I munch awhile upon a ham.
   Two dogs run by in chase,
The beach is stirred, and there I am
   With sand upon my face.

I grit my teeth and try a cheese.
   Some athletes with a ball,
Assisted also by the breeze,
   Raise up a sandy pall.

I turn to peanut butter now,
   But it is much the same. . . .
Oh, well, at least I've found out how
   The sandwich got its name.

I once managed to work two successive puns into the ending of a topical piece. The final one alone might have
sufficed, but the combination of the two produced, I believe, a more satisfying climax:

A STITCH IN TAMMANY

International Ladies Garment Workers Union Buys Tam-
many Hall.—*Newspaper headline.*

Where once the sacred tiger roared
   And petty bosses trembled,
Now seamstresses with cutting board
   And needle are assembled.

The order changeth, all transmutes,
   In life's unending serial:
Now ancient ghosts wear union suits
   And Tweed is a material.

And here is a *Sports Illustrated* poem that rests not on a
pun but on a comma:

GOOD LOOKING

It's not her figure skating that
Men find exhilarating.
No, what they're always looking at
Is just her figure, skating.

My belief in the importance of the ending, even at the expense of some other part of the poem, is indicated by the fact that I once sacrificed what seemed an unusually apt title in order to strengthen the last line. It was in this piece: .

DOGGED DETERMINATION

A dog is a creature for any boy
To love with a fiercely possessive joy,
For neighbors out of their yards to shoo,
For dogs of opposite sex to woo,
For other dogs in the night to bark at,
For would-be sleepers to rouse and hark at,
For cats and delivery men to beware of,
And dog-tired parents like me to take care of.

I had originally written the last line,

And patient parents like me to take care of,

and had given the poem *Dog Tired* as its title. But it seemed to me that the ending was a little too matter-of-fact. It needed an extra touch of the amusing. So I replaced the alliterative but commonplace word "patient" with the pun I had planned for my title, found another label for my poem, and was much better satisfied. It was a case of laying down a sacrifice to bring in a run. And it is runs that most of us are after.

CHAPTER SEVEN

Title Tattle

IF the idea is the content and the expression the package of a humorous poem, the title is its label. It is intended not merely to tell what is inside—in fact sometimes it avoids doing so for the sake of surprise—but to arouse enough interest to cause the package to be opened. And this is not all, for a title should do more than lure the reader into beginning. When the reading is completed, recognition of the aptness of the title should lend an additional touch of humor. On the practical side, this can have much to do with making a sale, particularly in a borderline case. Since a glance back at the title may give the editor his final impression of the poem, the cleverness of the title, its full import now appreciated, may move him to a favorable decision. From the standpoint of the writer, there is a strong temptation to feel that the job is done when the last line is written, and to slap onto the poem the first title that comes to mind. But the title is distinctly a part of the whole, and should not be slighted. The writer will do well to work as conscientiously on it as on his meter and rhymes. The label may, indeed, sell the product.

Inasmuch as light verse is usually brief, its titles are usually brief also. For one thing, short titles fit nicely into the narrow columns of most magazines. Whatever the reason, titles commonly consist of only one or two words, and seldom more than four or five. One exception is the case of a very short poem with a very long title, where humor is derived from the incongruity and from the reversal of the ordinary. The title, in such a case, is a kind of prologue to the poem, giving the background or explaining the situation. Here is an example of what I mean —a poem of nine words with a title of twelve:

A GARDENER'S OBSERVATION ON
THE TRULY TERRIBLE RESULTS
OF THE ORIGINAL SIN

There wasn't a weed in
The garden of Eden.

Part of the humor, such as it is, derives from the incongruity of the brief, simple couplet and the long, treatise-like title. But this is a *tour de force,* effective only occasionally.

Ogden Nash has a fondness for long titles of a double-barrelled sort, reminiscent of books of adventure combined with moral uplift, like those of Horatio Alger. They are, however, usually affixed to poems of better than average length for light verse. Random examples are his *Hearts of Gold; Or, A Good Excuse Is Worse than None* and his *Lines to a World-Famous Poet Who Failed to Complete a*

World-Famous Poem; Or, Come Clean, Mr. Guest! Phyllis McGinley, who also occasionally uses this technique, is more often inclined to add an explanatory subtitle or parenthetical remark, as in her *Song from New Rochelle [with a refrain to be chanted solemnly by a chorus consisting of N.Y., N.H. & Hartford R.R. conductors, passenger agents, and John Coolidge]*. To return to Ogden Nash, his specialty is the slightly insane title that perfectly matches his verse. Who but he could have written such titles as these: *To a Lady Passing Time Better Left Unpassed; Bankers Are Just Like Anybody Else, Only Richer; Suppose I Darken Your Door; Procrastination Is All of the Time;* and *You Cad, Why Don't You Cringe?* Like his poems, his titles are not for others to imitate.

Let me now run through some of the titles I have used for my own light verse and see whether I can explain why they were chosen. Sometimes it must have been because of alliteration, as *Music-Hall Musings* and *Calendar Comment,* or alliteration combined with some other similarity of sound, such as *Travel Travail*. Sometimes it was rhyme, as *Molar Dolors,* or a combination of rhyme and alliteration, as *Congressional Confessional*. Most often, I am sure, it was on account of some kind of wordplay. I admit a failing for puns in titles. But I think, and hope, that this is one place where puns are acceptable even to those who normally groan at them. Here are a few examples of different kinds of wordplay I have used in titles:

1. Coinages: *Anecdotage, Barberous.*

2. Split words: *Tale Spin, Auto Motive, Shop Worn.* (Splitting the word yuletide, and punning as well, gave me *Yule Tried.*)

3. Opposites: *Cup that Doesn't Cheer, What This Country Doesn't Need, Seeing Isn't Believing, Uncommon Garden Variety, A House Multiplied, No Sooner Done than Said.*

4. Puns on sayings or common expressions: *Toys Will Be Toys, Speed the Parting Gust, State of the Notion, All of a Peace, To Have and Too Old, No Youth Talking, Room and Bard.*

5. Miscellaneous puns and wordplay: *Daily Doesn't, News Buoy, Heavy Wait, Brothers Under My Skin, Bank Knight* (and the reverse, *Night of the Bath*), *Site Unseen, Two Bad, Winter Tailspin, How Green Is My Liver, What You Don't Know Won't Hurt You Till Later.*

It is in their application, however, that titles are effective or not. Thus *Stein Song* is nothing by itself, but it adds amusement to a poem about Gertrude Stein. *Viewed with Alarm* is a common expression that takes on new meaning as the title of a poem about alarm clocks. And *End of a Slack Season* similarly becomes more than it seemed at first glance when linked with these lines:

> Hasten, summer, speed your ending,
> Welcome, fall, toward which we're tending,
>
> A saner season, thank the Lord,
> When two-piece slack suits will be stored,
>
> And shirttails will be worn by men
> Inside their trousers once again.

Would you like to test your own inventiveness? Put yourself in the position of the writer of the quatrain that follows. What title would you have chosen for it?

> "Come on," they said, "let's double up
> And all go in our car."
> Now we are in, and you should see
> How doubled up we are.

You might play with the word "double" in something like *Double or Nothing* or *Double Trouble*. Or you might try "bent" in *Pleasure Bent*. Or you could describe the ridiculous situation, as I did in the title I finally used, *Would You Mind Taking Your Elbow Out of My Ear?*

In the same way, you might see what you could think up as a label for this little piece:

> This crux, this dilemma, this crisis is one
> With which many nights I have reckoned:
> To stay in bed cold with one blanket or else
> Get up in the cold for a second.

After considering the alliterative *Blankety Blank* and *Chilly Choice,* and the punning *Bed of Ruses,* I decided upon the alliterative pun of *Cold Comfort.*

If you like this kind of game, here is one more for you:

> Citronella and various lotions
> That cause mosquitoes to fear you
> Arouse, it happens, the same emotions
> In persons who chance to be near you.

How about *Distance Lends Enchantment?* Or *Smear Campaign?* The best I could do, when I wrote the poem, was *Odor of the Day.*

I am sometimes happier about a title than about the poem itself. Of course I am happiest when I feel that the title is exactly right for the poem to which it is attached.

In my prejudiced opinion, *Pique of Perfection,* which follows, is a well-labelled poem. At any rate, in the years since it was published I have not thought of a better title for it. All too often it turns out otherwise. What especially chagrins me is to think of a definitely superior title just after I have dropped my poem in the postbox.

PIQUE OF PERFECTION

A man of 38 is in the peak period of his mental powers, but his physical condition has been slowly declining from the high point reached at around 25.—*News item.*

> When I was five and twenty,
>   And sportively inclined,
> I had physique aplenty
>   But very little mind,
>
> Whereas, now grown maturer,
>   And all of thirty-eight,
> My mental powers are surer
>   But, oh, my body's state!
>
> A sage whose pace is slowing
>   Supplants the virile dunce.
> There seems no way of knowing
>   The best of me at once.

The suggestion of Housman in the opening, by the way, reminds me of David McCord's *A Stropshire Lad,* which I intend to quote in a subsequent chapter. Now *there* is a title for you. It fills me with admiration and envy.

Frequently a title comes to me before I have a poem to go with it. This means that I must file it away until I have a poem it will fit, or, as sometimes happens, get to work to build a poem around it. Occasionally I conjure up a title that seems to me so good—although it may not be half so appealing to others—that I am tempted to use it more than once. This is obviously not sound practice, particularly when two or more poems of the same title are submitted to the same magazine. But I have succumbed to the temptation at least once, in the case of *Sinus of Spring*. My only justification was a decorous lapse of time between the first poem of this name and the second. It may also happen that, after titling a poem, I discover that someone else has already used my title, although perhaps in quite a different sense. Unless I make the discovery too late, and my poem has already been sent out, the only thing to do is to substitute another title, however reluctantly. Not long ago I had to give up *Auto Suggestion* and replace it with *Auto Motive,* which meant losing a certain amount of aptness. Likewise, discovery that Margaret Fishback had earlier employed *Lines of Lease Resistance* forced me to use *Lease Majesty* for the poem I quoted a few pages back. It is fine to love your own titles. However, it is not sensible to cling to them stubbornly when they are found to have been preempted, or when you feel that they may be missed, or misconstrued, by the reader.

I do not mean to overemphasize. The titling of poems is a little like the naming of one's children. Fortunately for both poets and parents, if the poem or the child has sufficient character, it will get along all right in the world, regardless of what it is called.

CHAPTER EIGHT

That Blank Look

STARTING is such sweet sorrow. With the best intentions, you may find it hard to set down the first words. A stoppage of some sort seems to keep the ideas from flowing. You may blame it on the fact that you are a beginner and have not yet written enough to get in the swing. Or on the fact that you have been turning the stuff out for years, and are finally running low on ideas and creative energy. Some consolation may be derived from the knowledge that others, both tyros and veterans, also find it difficult to get under way. But this is slight comfort when what you really want is a vigorous push past those first few words. It *is* a problem. The few suggestions I hopefully offer are based on personal experience, and may be of little or no value to others.

A blank piece of paper has an hypnotic effect on me. Its emptiness seems to reflect itself on my mind. The result is sometimes a feeling of defeat and despondency, sometimes of drowsiness. This latter, if not shaken off, leads to pleasant but unproductive sleep. The only preventive remedy I have found is the strict avoidance of blank paper until such time as the words start coming. That is why I prefer to commence with a discarded piece of paper that has some handwriting or typing on it. If nothing of the sort is available, I write down on the unsullied sheet a few random words. Frequently this aimless scribbling is itself productive of an idea which, if not usable, often leads to one that is. Ideas will set each other off like firecrackers in a bunch. It is simply a matter of somehow igniting the first of them. From then on, things take care of themselves.

An idea is of course the most usual, and in many ways the most desirable, thing to start with. You must have an idea before you finish your poem, even though you do not precisely have it at the outset. If you possess one to start with, you can then turn all your efforts to its presentation, and not still be groping around for something to say while endeavoring to say it. Frequently, as you sit before your piece of paper, you will recall some incident of the present or of a previous day, and so take your idea directly from life. For example, a losing tussle with a drinking fountain gave me the concluding line of the following poem, which I developed immediately after the occurrence.

INSCRIPTION FOR A DRINKING FOUNTAIN

Let handles turn and valves release,
Let flowing start and leaking cease,
Let pipes pipe well, and filters filter,
Let no small part be out of kilter.
Let tepid water run off fast,
Let cooler liquid come at last,

And be it free from things that squirm,
Both seen and microscopic germ.
Come, let the crystal geyser mount,
Come on, old fountain, up and fount,
But do not bubble, burp, and blow,
Or vacillate 'twixt high and low.
Please keep a steady, decent pace:
I did not come to wash my face.

And the varied reactions to a new photograph, my first in more than ten years, led me to write the following lines:

Unreasonable Facsimile

Unfailingly my photograph
Is one at which observers laugh
Or say, and quite indignantly,
It doesn't look a bit like me.
Which proves (and I have searched my heart)
Photographers have lost their art,
Or else, and here the matter ends,
I'm blest with loyal, lying friends.

It may, however, be necessary to imagine, to invent. If you can think up something that quite plausibly could have happened to you, and that may very well have happened to others, it will be every bit as good for your purpose.

What if the full-blown idea does not come? I sometimes toy with rhymes until I discover one that seems to me fresh and interesting. With this as a basis, I may then be able to develop a couplet, a quatrain, or a longer poem. When I have finished, the rhyme may be in the opening line or in the last line. Or it may, in a couplet or quatrain, be virtually the whole poem. Just so, the rhyme *glasses-grass is,* which probably arose out of a reminiscence of Dorothy Parker's *passes-glasses,* prompted this couplet:

DARK OUTLOOK IN HOLLYWOOD

Girls who always wear dark glasses
Never know how green the grass is.

A rhyme that I had used once before, in a very different context, was the foundation upon which I constructed the following quatrain:

SPEAKING OF CHILDREN

When parents commence
   On their children's precocity,
I'd like to go hence
   With the utmost velocity.

Equally useful as a point of departure is play with words. Despite the fact that I was, admittedly, fighting a chairborne war in an Army headquarters, it was not my observation of the activity or inactivity around me, but an accidental pairing of the words "headquarters" and "hindquarters," that produced:

THE OLD ARMY GAME

This, I declare,
   I am standing pat on:
Headquarters is where
   Hindquarters are sat on.

In like manner, in both the title and the pay-off last line, I made use of the double meaning of a word in:

Occupied

Peering above,
Probing beneath,
Curling her lashes,
Brushing her teeth,

Daubing her face
With every new mixture,
Our teen-age daughter's
A bathroom fixture.

I have done the same sort of thing with "spare bedroom," "open mind," and many another. In each case I had no real idea to start with, but the suggestive word or phrase invariably led me to one.

Still another good opening wedge is an axiom or common saying. Looked at long enough, first this way and then that, it is very likely to suggest a new twist or a barbed comment. Here is an instance of turning a familiar expression inside out:

Worth Waiting For

I hope I'm alive on the day
  Some honest chap precedent shatters
By saying, "It isn't the principle,
  It's only the money that matters."

Similarly, a little cogitation over "beauty is only skin deep" evoked this comment on the old adage:

Depth Charge

That beauty's only skin deep may
  Be true as true can be,

But who's complaining, anyway?
It's plenty deep for me.

As times goes on, one is certain to accumulate a "bone pile"—a folder of odds and ends of discarded titles and rhymes, abortive opening lines, and whole poems that call for redoing in a more inspired or patient mood. It is to such a scrapheap that I resort at those times when I am utterly barren of ideas and incapable either of thinking up a new rhyme or indulging in word play. There is a chance, however slim, that I may now be in the frame of mind to build a skeleton out of these old bones, and maybe even put some flesh on them, dress them up, and send them out with the living. If not, I can at least spend my minutes well by classifying these relics and discarding some of the more obviously useless in order to make the hunting easier next time.

The bone pile availing me nothing, I usually turn through a volume of Ogden Nash, Dorothy Parker, Arthur Guiterman, Phyllis McGinley, Margaret Fishback, Morris Bishop, David McCord, or some anthology in which I will find these favorites represented along with others. I do this reluctantly, because there is always the danger that I shall become engrossed, and give all of my slender quota of writing time to the easier business of reading. To forestall any such escape from the task at hand, I frequently set myself a certain time, say half an hour, after which I must close my book and return to the still untouched sheet of paper. I could cite many instances of how the reading of others' verses has stimulated my thinking and provided me with ideas. Typical is the way Ogden Nash's lines on the inevitable growth of kittens gave me the cue for:

NATURAL DEVELOPMENT

One dreadful truth I rather wish
I did not know is that
The woman who is kittenish
Will one day be a cat.

I have already remarked on how Margaret Fishback's *To a Young Man Selecting Six Orchids* started me off on my own *Lines for a Young Man Going Calling,* and how recollections of Gelett Burgess and Samuel Hoffenstein and Arthur Guiterman had their part in the shaping of other poems. If suggestions can be borrowed without taking over complete ideas, this purposeful reading can be of much value to the temporarily inert mind. But again I caution against allowing reading to supplant writing.

There is always the newspaper. Careful study of headlines and promising news items in the morning paper may either furnish a new thought or fan into fire one that has been smoldering in the subconscious. Often there will be a headline or a sentence that can be commented on satirically or in some way played with. I am continually on the lookout for these. What I want is not a "newsbreak," such as *The New Yorker* prints, with a wry editorial note, at the bottom of its pages. Instead of being obviously amusing in itself, the item must have the possibility of being worked into something amusing. Part of the reader's enjoyment in this kind of topical verse comes from his following the development of a thought that is wrung out of what did not appear to be very promising material. A couple of examples may make my point clearer.

Making Light of It

The American Home Lighting Institute says that good lighting can do more to improve a woman's looks than the most expensive cosmetics.—*News item.*

Girls, if you would catch a man
    And win a cozy cottage,
You'll find that it will help your plan
    If you will watch the wattage.

Yes, watch the watt and check the amp,
    It seems a man will sit up
If you sit down beside a lamp
    That makes you nicely lit up.

For ugly shadows cast about
    Can double up the chin line
And make those features look more stout
    Where there should be a thin line.

Poor light may make the smartest type
    Look immature and callow,
May even make one look unripe
    And slightly green and sallow.

Turn lights up high, don't turn them low,
    Though it's at first upsetting.
Your eyes will sparkle, skin will glow,
    And he'll know what he's getting.

And then there is this, a gruesome little piece that has been a good deal reprinted and is a favorite of mine:

Hiding Place

A speaker at a meeting of the New York State Frozen Food Locker Association declared that the best hiding place in event of an atomic explosion is a frozen-food locker, where "radiation will not penetrate."—*News item.*

> Move over, ham
>   And quartered cow,
> My Geiger says
>   The time is now.
>
> Yes, now I lay me
>   Down to sleep,
> And if I die,
>   At least I'll keep.

The newspaper is a wonderful mirror of the absurd antics of humanity. It is therefore a steady source of ideas. The only trouble with verse based upon what we call a "news peg" is that in a few weeks or months it may be as dated as the incident that inspired it. But it is sometimes possible to develop a current topic in such a way as to emphasize the timeless and universal. The headlines may change, but human nature remains much the same.

Anyhow, a bit of topical verse may serve to start the ideas flowing and to limber up the meters. Anything to get going.

CHAPTER NINE

Easy Doesn't It

VERY few persons find writing of any kind either easy or pleasant. So powerful is the allure of alternatives—reading or golfing or playing bridge or talking to a friend—that it is a wonder any writing is ever done. However, there is no disputing the fact that a considerable amount of it *is* done by the relatively few who have the urge to embark upon it and the will power to stay with it. Indeed, people fall into one or the other of two classes—those who write and those who merely want to—in accordance with the strength or weakness of this urge and this will power. Whether they publish what they write depends on a few other qualities, such as ability or talent, and maybe a little luck. But it chiefly depends on unflagging industry and on perseverance in the face of repeated rebuffs. In other words, urge and will power again.

Light verse is no exception. For all the fun it may give the reader, it is seldom unalloyed fun to write. Of course there is less investment of time and effort than in writing a novel or a short story. The job can be done in odd moments. Since the time from beginning to completion is relatively brief, it is not long until the work is finished and the writer has that happy sensation of accomplishment, which lasts until he becomes impatient to get on with the next project. Light verse is without doubt easier to write than any other literary form: it requires less planning, less study, less sustaining of emotion. Yet, except for those occasional pieces that come to one fully formed, it is work also. And these exceptional pieces that seem to come without effort would not have put in their appearance at all had there not been a previous stirring up of the mind and perhaps a few vexatious trials and errors. This may seem to be laboring an obvious point, but it comes from the heart. How often some well-meaning person has exclaimed to me, about a piece of verse I struggled hard over, "My, you must have had fun writing that!" But my flash of irritation quickly gives way to flattered pleasure, because I know that light verse should read as though written with fun, whatever the actual labor of composition.

The steady output of light verse, like the quantity production of any writing, is virtually impossible unless one has acquired the writing habit. There must be a schedule of some sort, and this schedule must be rigidly adhered to. If the writing of light verse is a part-time occupation, as it usually is, one may contend that it is not feasible to set aside a definite period each day. The chances are, however, that an hour or two can be found in the early morning or late evening despite other breadwinning or social activities. If definiteness of hours cannot be managed, there can at any rate be the regularity of writing a little bit each day. Establishment of this regularity is of the first importance. Once the forced routine becomes a habit, the writer is really on his way. It is a haunting, plaguing thing, this writing habit. One who has it is likely to look with envy at those who are blissfully free from it, and who may be bound only by the relatively frail bonds of alcohol or tobacco. It is hard to live with and hard to write without. It is annoying and wearing and it often turns one into an unsocial being, but it is a virtual guarantee that some writing will be done.

Aside from regularity, there is nothing quite so important as frequency of writing. Yesterday's idea may be today's poem. Left until the day after tomorrow, it may sink to the bottom of the subconscious and stubbornly refuse to be dragged up to the surface again. A lapse of a week, instead of proving a refreshment and a stimulus, will in all probability cause a setback. I have long since given up waiting for an inspiration. My own experience is that ideas for verses come most readily when I am most unrelentingly in pursuit of them. And I am sure that facility of phrasing improves with practice and deteriorates with idleness. Unlike the rapidly rotating stone that accumulates no moss, a writer must keep rolling in order to gather greenbacks.

When one is not writing, one may be busy preparing to do so. The human comedy can be unceasingly scanned for ideas, and these notes can be jotted down in the notebook that should always be within reach. One need not lie awake nights trying to contrive rhymes, although the light verse writer is likely to become acquainted with the tossings and turnings of insomnia, but one should keep pencil and paper at the bedside, and be ready to capture the evanescent thought that lingers briefly at waking. More than once, when no light was handy, I have written down a few lines in the darkness, and hoped I could read them in the morning. When it turned out that I had scribbled on a page that had already been written on, the deciphering was somewhat more difficult than usual.

Another sort of preparation, which I have mentioned before, is reading—not only light verse but literature, and especially poetry, of all kinds. I have been struck repeatedly by the evidence of wide reading apparent in the poems of some of our most popular contemporary light verse writers. They seem to have read widely and remembered well, as is evidenced by the verse forms they use, by verbal reminiscences, and by outright allusions. Take David McCord, one of the most literate as well as proficient. His easy familiarity with the English poets is one of the delights of his skillful parody of Housman, the title of which I have already cited.

A Stropshire Lad

"Experience has taught me, when I am shaving of a morning, to keep watch over my thoughts, because, if a line of poetry strays into my memory, my skin bristles so that the razor ceases to act."—A. E. Housman in *The Name and Nature of Poetry*.

> When I was one and twenty,
>   With down upon the chin,
> A little soap was plenty
>   As daily I'd begin.

Then reading Blake and William
   From dark to dewy morn,
I sprang up like a trillium
   Amid the Ludlow corn;

And like the starry gazer,
   Myself would wrap in thought
And let the ragged razor
   Attend me as it ought.

With foamy lips, and mouthy
   Of Latin verbs and Greek,
I'd say a little Southey
   And shave the other cheek.

But now that I am bristled,
   Needs I must quote with care:
For one as over-thistled
   There's little skin to spare.

By silly prose and blather
   I'll not be troubled much,
But lads are hell for lather
   Who think of poems and such.

So Collins, Smart, and Cowper
   And him of lovely bars
I swear at like a trooper,
   And furrow fresh the scars.

Nor is this reading I recommend solely, or even usually, to gain the background for parodies. It is more to pick up rhythms and nuances of wit and humor from the masters, and to learn what can be done with ideas and words.

Demanding as is the initial writing of a piece of light

verse, an even larger measure of patience and industry is required when it comes to revision. It is in the working over, the final polishing of a poem, that the craftsmanship of the artist or the artistry of the craftsman is given its real test. How hard it is to tear apart, in order to build better, what was already passably good! How hard it is to stay a little longer with the finished piece, when a new and momentarily more engaging idea is at hand to commence upon! Moreover, one must often be one's own critic. Friends are too busy with their own work, or too kind in their comments, to be helpfully critical. First-class literary agents, sometimes useful advisers to writers of novels and short stories, will not be bothered with relatively unre- munerative verse. Second-class literary agents are a waste of time and money. Once in a while, of course, an editor will return a poem and suggest some sort of revision, after which he will be glad to have a second look. But this is only when the poem was almost good enough in its original form. Not long ago I submitted to a magazine a poem that opened with this stanza:

> While at a party which, I pout,
> They almost had to bind me
> To get me to, I muse about
> The girl I left behind me.

I had misgivings when I sent it off. I knew that it was hard to read—harder probably for others than for me, since I knew what I wanted to say. But because of what was to follow, I felt that the last line of this stanza must remain as it was. And within the self-imposed limitations of rhyme and meter, I thought I could do no better. So I let it go. Of course it came back. However, instead of giving me an outright rejection, the editor said, "The first stanza seems to us awkward. Could you smooth it out and let us see it again?" I had worked hard over it before, and had seen no way to retain the line I wanted and yet make the reading smooth. Nevertheless, I had another go at it. As usual, it *could* be done a bit better. It simply took a little more trying. With the first stanza revised and the rest of the poem unchanged, back it went. This time it stuck. Here is the way it appeared when published:

HOME GUARD

Against my will I was dragged out
  And at a party find me,
Where ruefully I muse about
  The girl I left behind me.

And as the evening wears (and wears),
  I hourly grow more bitter
To think of how my lot compares
  With hers—the baby sitter.

She is the mistress of my home
  As soon as I've departed.
Not made, like me, perforce to roam,
  She reads the book I'd started.

Upon the radio she hears
  The programs I am missing.
My records, gathered through the years,
  She plays, while reminiscing.

While I hide yawns as best I can
  At talk not of my choosing,

> She stretches out on my divan
> And does a little snoozing.
>
> But what is just too much for me
> And turns me really sour
> Is that it isn't I, but she,
> Who gets paid by the hour!

This was one time when I was fortunate enough to get an opportunity to revise. How many times my poem was not quite good enough or the editor not quite kindhearted enough to give me such a second chance, I cannot guess. Such an incident makes me determined to revise with greater care and to be satisfied less easily.

Yes, there is work, perhaps more than meets the eye, in the writing of light verse as in any kind of writing. It is much more pleasant to do a thousand other things, to procrastinate from day to day and month to month. Bert Leston Taylor expresses the feelings of most of us in *The Lazy Writer:*

> In summer I'm disposed to shirk,
> As summer is no time to work.
>
> In winter inspiration dies
> For lack of outdoor exercise.
>
> In spring I'm seldom in the mood
> Because of vernal lassitude.
>
> The fall remains. But such a fall!
> We've really had no fall at all.

CHAPTER TEN

To Market, To Market

LIKE a man with a new joke to tell, the writer with a just-completed piece of light verse can be expected to start looking around for an audience. In this respect light verse writers are probably different from serious poets, a fair proportion of whom may, indeed, write only for their own satisfaction, and tuck their poems away in a desk pigeonhole or a carefully locked diary. It is true that an emotional catharsis may be gained from writing unpublished lines that air a grudge against some phase of life or certain kinds of people. For the most part, however, light verse is meant to be communicated and appreciated. It is normal for the writer to wish others to read it, and to be happy when they are amused. If the audience is the many readers of a magazine instead of the few members of his household, so much the better. And then there is the financial return. Undoubtedly much light verse has been motivated by the prospect of monetary reward. But I

114

doubt that this matters greatly, or that anyone could be sure which lines were written for posterity and which for the purse. Whether it is art for art's sake or for the artist's is not of great moment, so long as the art is there.

Assuming, then, that you want to publish your light verse and get paid for it, how do you go about it? Most important is the matter of knowing your markets: which magazines and newspapers use light verse, and what kind they prefer. There is more to this than is at first apparent.

To start with, one should get hold of a rather complete list of markets. One of the most exhaustive of these will be found in *The Writer's Handbook,* edited by A. S. Burack. Since all the periodicals that print poetry are usually grouped under one heading, the editorial comments and requirements should be read carefully in order to determine which magazines actually use light, humorous verse. It is worth while also to scan other groups, such as those headed "Humor," "Juveniles," and "Trade and Business Magazines," on the chance that here too there may be openings for light verse. For convenient reference, it is suggested that the names and addresses of the most likely magazines and papers be copied into what will become your own working list of markets. This can subsequently be kept up to date through changes indicated by monthly notes published in such magazines as *The Writer* and *Writer's Digest.* As these markets are tried, and sales are made or poems are returned, further alterations can be made and the list kept alive and useful. By the way, the comment "no verse" that appears in the thumbnail write-ups of many magazines should not be taken too seriously. Often it means "no run-of-the-mine sentimental or nature poetry." A clever piece of light verse may be quite acceptable. My personal list of most-tried markets presently numbers eighteen, though I have written for more than two hundred. I keep working this list over, pruning out the deadwood.

Helpful as are the comments that accompany most printed lists, they are no substitute for actual examination of the magazines in question. It is a good investment of money to buy an occasional copy of the various periodicals that use light verse, and a good investment of time to study the kind of verse they print, as well as their general tone. This "getting the feel" of the magazine is almost as profitable as a talk with the editor. In fact, if you could get in to see him he would be almost certain to remark, sooner or later: "I suggest that you study our magazine." From this study you will be able to decide whether your type of writing will fit a given market, and whether you have something on hand that you might submit to it. You can also determine what sort of subject and treatment will be called for in your future work if you are scheming to crash its pages.

Gradually you will learn what it is that magazines generally want and what are the specific requirements of particular markets. You will find, for instance, that there are all sorts of taboos. Some editors, because of their readership, will not accept a poem that makes a reference, even facetiously, to liquor. Others shy away from excessive use of slang. I have run into one editor who has a violent allergy against allergies—poems about hay fever especially. Another, I am sure, dislikes poems about children. In his kindly way, he says that he is overstocked with such poems, but I have never known him to print anything from that supposedly bulging supply.

One of the things to be learned is the length of poem that each magazine customarily publishes. Some like two- and four-line poems to fill up the odd spaces. Others consider these too slight, and prefer something more substantial. Some have a strict rule against poems of over, say, twenty lines. (But no such rule, I have found, is ironclad.) Others will take a poem that fills an entire page, sometimes featuring it and pointing it up with illustrative drawings around the border. Generally speaking, short poems are more acceptable than long ones. By short I mean from two to a dozen lines. Also to be discovered is the dominant interest of the magazine, such as the women-home-family theme of *Good Housekeeping* and *Family Weekly*; the sophisticated, often satirical bent of *The New Yorker*; the timely accent in *The Wall Street Journal*. Most likely to appeal to the editor is the poem that has freshness of theme and expression, is of a length that will fit nicely into the allotted space, and is of the type that will appeal generally to the magazine's readers. First-hand knowledge of magazines saves time and postage. Moreover, it improves your standing with editors when you do not bother them with material that is obviously wide of the mark.

A few words now about the mechanics of submitting poems. It goes without saying that manuscripts should be neat. They should be typewritten, double-spaced, on standard-size typewriter paper. The typewriter keys should be kept clean and the ribbon well inked. A manuscript has the look of a careless amateur when the capitals drop half a line below the other letters, and the "a," "e," and "o" are so clogged as to be indistinguishable round smudges.

It takes very little longer to center a poem on the page than to set it down any old place. The same goes for centering the lines under the title, which should be made to stand out through the use of capitals or underlining. But no fancy tricks. No drawings in the margins—unless they are an integral part of the poem and meant to be reproduced. Just the look of regularity and cleanness which makes reading easy and which, if it does not in itself sell the poem, at least does not hamper the sale by making a bad impression. The name and return address should appear plainly on each sheet of paper, customarily in the upper left-hand corner. And of course a stamped, self-addressed envelope should be enclosed. Without it, your poems may still be sent back to you, a few times at least. But that is not the way to make friends and influence editors.

You may submit one poem at a time, or half a dozen. So far as I know, it makes little difference. The single poem may stand out better, all by itself, but the one-at-a-time method uses up postage rapidly and makes the editor do a good deal of note writing or inserting of rejection slips into envelopes. However, if a single poem is ready and has no fit companions, and especially if delay would mar its timeliness, by all means shoot it off.

Sometimes short poems on the same general topic can be grouped and submitted for publication together. The cumulative effect of the whole may do what any one of the parts, singly, would not have done. This is true of the following group of couplets about glasses:

THE EYES HAVE IT

Two things seldom in one place:
One's glasses and one's glasses case.

The time a fellow needs some friends is
When he's broken both his lenses.

As years go by, one yearns aplenty
For youth and good old 20/20.

I have used the same collective method with couplets and quatrains about such motley subjects as kisses, assorted relishes, elevators, and real estate. Sometimes only three or four of half a dozen submitted parts have been purchased, but there might otherwise have been no sale at all.

The light verse writer needs to keep a calendar handy, and to understand the importance of the time of the year in submitting his poems. Let us imagine that it is the middle of July. You have just come back from your vacation at the beach. What you saw and heard as you sunbathed on the sand now begins to emerge in the form of poems about lifeguards and sunburn and resort hotels and the human figure and children who dig holes for adults to fall into. Your poems are written and polished and ready to send to market. Do not forget to look at that calendar. The large-circulation monthly magazines, such as *Good Housekeeping*, probably have their September number ready for mailing to subscribers, and their October number well along. They could not print your pieces until November at the earliest. And they are probably not yet in the mood to buy for next summer's issues.

Although many of the weekly magazines that once bought light verse are no longer being published, there are a number of alternative markets that should be explored; for example, the daily and weekly newspapers, Sunday supplements, trade journals, regional magazines, and religious publications. These are good markets for timely or general material. If the topic of your poem is so timely that other writers may also have chosen it, or if you feel that it may be out of date soon, send it out now. Editors will never turn down good light verse, even though they may have to hold it for several months before the appropriate month or season. If you can plan ahead, figure three to five months before publication.

But remember that publishing schedules and editors' buying habits vary so greatly that this is something that can be learned only by experience. The ideal, of course, is to contrive for your poem to reach the editor early enough for him to be able to fit it into an appropriate forthcoming issue, and late enough for him to be interested in the future season or event to which it has reference. Intelligent timing pays—time and time again.

When a poem is mailed out, some sort of record should be kept of where it is. This is to safeguard against the rare case of loss and to insure that the same poem is not sold to two magazines, which would be most embarrassing. The record can be very simple. Some writers enter the title of each poem, and note its peregrinations, on a three-by-five card. My method is still simpler, though perhaps somewhat less efficient. I note in the upper right-hand corner of my retained copy of the poem the place to which it was sent. If it comes back, I make a check mark by the name of the magazine that returned it, and indicate the one to which it is next submitted just below. If it sells, I note on the bottom of the sheet the name of the magazine to which it was sold, and what sum it brought. In one folder I keep the "To Sell," in another the "Out," and in a third the "Sold." When my poems appear in print, I clip them and paste them in scrapbooks. These books of clippings give me a chronological record of publications and an authentic source of the final text, in the event there were any last-minute changes. It is to such scrapbooks that one may easily refer if occasion arises to compile a collection of one's verse, or to make a little talk before the Ladies' Literary Circle.

I try to keep forty or fifty poems always in the mail, and have pushed the number up as high as a hundred. If two come back, two go out. If six come back, six go out. This requires a considerable amount of typing and bookkeeping. The more time that is given to maintenance of records, the less that remains for writing. So the system of recording and checking must be as labor-saving as possible.

A final word about rejections. A printed rejection slip, however politely worded, is an unlovely thing. It is bound to bring with it a moment of disappointment, perhaps of anger at the editor who failed to recognize superior quality. But if the emotion is translated into determination rather than despair, it can be a stimulus to renewed effort. I believe in the method of erosion—gradually wearing editors down, never relenting. After a while the monotonous stream of rejection slips will be broken by a few words of encouragement: "Keep at it." "Close. Try again." "Almost made it that time. Send some more." And then, one day, you ring the bell. But let no one think that one sale, or a hundred sales, to a certain market insures the acceptance of one's next piece. It helps to have got in. It helps to be on the editor's list of good prospects. Yet the writer's name will not sell a really inferior product. Conversely, a superior piece of light verse from an unknown will almost certainly be purchased. So far as I have been able to discover, everything gets a reading in the editorial offices. The best poems are passed along until they come to the editor who is empowered to give the final yes or no that means a check or a rejection slip. I have come to have great respect for the judgment of editors. After all, it is their business to know what is publishable. If they are not profound literary critics, they at least know what their magazine is driving at and what their readers want.

Even if an editor turns your poem down, that does not mean that it is hopelessly bad. It may mean that it was not quite suitable for that particular magazine. So send it to another of different type. It may mean that there was some rough spot in its handling, or a lack of punch. So get busy with the revision. It may mean that it reached the magazine too late for use in the present season and too early to be stored for the next. So send it to a newspaper, or hold it over until the following season. It may mean that someone else has beaten you to it on the same subject. So chalk it up to experience, and try to be a little quicker next time. However, repeated rejection of a poem probably means that it simply is not good enough, in the face of stiff competition. So chuck it. A piece of paper with a beaten-down poem on it can be put to no better use than as the worksheet for a new one—one (and you are *sure* of it this time) that they will find it impossible to resist!

CHAPTER ELEVEN

Anyone for Prose?

HUMOR is humor, whether in verse or prose. Those who for one reason or another have had no great success with writing and publishing light verse, but who have an eye for the absurdities of life, might give prose humor a try. And those who have succeeded with light verse might, without giving it up, widen their range by writing prose humor also.

It helps the writer of prose, I think, to have written verse, whether light verse or serious poetry. The reason for this is that verse writing requires more attention to the individual word than prose. Words must be chosen not only for their meaning and connotation but for their texture. To a verse writer, there are many agonizing decisions over whether to use this word or that. Words are not only long and short but light and heavy, rough and smooth. Words must be fitted together as stones are fitted together by a mason.

A writer I once knew was writing a biography of an eighteenth-century English dramatist. He told me that every morning before he began to write he read for about fifteen minutes from a little book called *The Beauties of Shakespeare,* a collection of some of the best passages from Shakespeare's plays. "It sharpens my feeling for words," he said. "It lifts the level of my vocabulary." So even if one does not write verse, the reading of verse (poetry) can have a tonic effect on one's writing of prose.

I might add that this man who honed his prose on *The Beauties of Shakespeare* won a prize for his biography, which was singled out and praised for its prose style.

Of the well-known light verse writers, not many write, or publish, prose humor. Ogden Nash, for example, sticks pretty much to his last (a last in which he is first), though his delightful, original light verse has of recent years expanded into the field of books for children. One of his rare pieces of prose is the foreword he wrote for my own *On Your Marks: A Package of Punctuation,* a book in verse on the punctuation marks. When he was approached about this, he said that he had an iron-clad rule against writing forewords or introductions. He had never written one and had no intention of breaking his rule. But he asked for a look at the manuscript, changed his mind, and wrote what I later told him was "the best page in the book." He could write prose humor—articles and books—if he wanted to.

Phyllis McGinley, however, after writing light verse for all the leading magazines, collecting her verses in a number of books, and winning the Pulitzer Prize for poetry, wrote the best-selling prose book, *Sixpence in Her Shoe.* And she has long written articles for magazines, usually in a light-serious vein and mostly about home and family. Her prose has the same delicacy of touch and precise choice of words as her superb light verse.

I have myself written both light verse and prose humor almost from the start. Of recent years I have increased the proportion of prose, partly because there is a wider market for prose and partly because I have begun to run low on ideas for verse. Since it is short, and since each piece of verse should have a new idea or a fresh approach to an old one, light verse uses up ideas fast. As I write this, I find I have passed the six thousand mark in the number of verses sold. How many new ideas and fresh approaches are there? I am beginning to think there is a limited number for any one person, certainly for me, but other minds will discover, or uncover, more thousands.

I *think* I write prose humor better because I also write light verse, although this is impossible to tell. Had I had two careers, one writing only prose and one writing both verse and prose, I could have compared the two. But whether or not I write prose any better, of one thing I am sure: I write it shorter. The brevity, the spareness of light verse has I am sure carried over to my prose. I was a long-winded, roundabout writer of prose during the years before I began to devote most of my waking, and some of my sleeping, hours to light verse. It may be only a coincidence, but my prose pieces now are shorter. I suppose this is good, but sometimes I wonder. After all, I get paid by the word or by the page.

Anyhow, humorous prose, though it is longer than light verse, should also be rather brief. Just as the most market-able piece of light verse is from a couplet to a dozen or so lines, the most salable piece of prose humor is probably from fifteen hundred to twenty-five hundred words. I have had the best luck with magazine pieces that ran six to eight typewritten pages, and rarely over ten. These were articles that found their way into magazines as various as *Parents'* and *Playboy, Saturday Review* and *The Reader's Digest.* Either it is hard for a writer of humor to sustain the mood very long, or the reader wears out—let us hope from laughing.

A book of humor should, I think, be hard to put down, but it should also be easy to pick up. Of course one of the greatest works of American humor, *Huckleberry Finn,* is a substantial book. But it is a work of genius, and as such can break all the rules. Also there is much in it besides humor.

And now, if you are ready, let us close in on the writing of prose humor, considering subjects to write about and approaches and writing techniques. At least you will have no need for a rhyming dictionary.

CHAPTER TWELVE

What Can You Be Funny About?

JUST about everything is grist for the humor writer's mill, including, I suppose, the word "grist," as well as mills, millers (see Chaucer), windmills (see Cervantes), and millstones. With humor, as with any kind of writing, you should write about what will be most interesting to your readers. If your readers were dogs, you would write about what is most interesting to dogs: lamp posts, fireplugs, dog food, and other dogs. But in all likelihood your readers will be people, and what people are most interested in is people.

About as universal a subject as you can find is the human body. Everybody, even a nobody, has a body, and the body —not the body beautiful but the body unbeautiful—has plenty of possibilities for humor. H. Allen Smith, for instance, wrote a very funny piece called "A Short History of Fingers," later included in a book with the same title. One of Corey Ford's most successful works, *How to Guess Your Age,* is a humorous treatment of the decline and fall of the human body.

I have written playful articles on hair, feet, ears, the nose, and other parts of the anatomy. In fact, I have become such a specialist that in "A Short Dissertation on Lips," published in *Playboy,* I concentrated on the lower lip. I may yet write an article on the upper lip, once I have done enough research on the subject.

Another *Playboy* article was "Looking Over the Overlooked Elbow." What intrigued me was that the elbow and the knee are joints that bend in opposite directions. I speculated at some length on what would happen if the two were reversed, the knee bending forward and the elbow bending back. This led me to so many other thoughts about the elbow from both aesthetic and utilitarian standpoints that I soon had two or three thousand words on the subject. After the article was published, a noted psychiatrist wrote me a letter—not finding anything wrong with me but suggesting that I write with equal erudition about the downtrodden, or trodden on, toe. I took his suggestion and wrote "Consider the Toe" (I also thought of calling it "On Your Toes") for another magazine.

The important thing, I believe, is to select a small but universal subject and develop it, rather than write briefly and superficially about a large subject. In humor, part of the fun is seeing something inconsequential developed by the ingenuity and imagination of the author. The very overdevelopment may lead to the absurdity which, properly handled, is basic in a great deal of humor.

Let me give you an example. I suppose as small a subject

as I have turned into a humorous article is the word, if you can call it a word, " 'n' "—as is used in "fish 'n' chips," "wash 'n' wear," etc. I wrote a deadpan, pseudo-scholarly article on this subject for the *Saturday Review,* going into all possible ramifications of the subject, including the tendency to leave out the second apostrophe, making it " 'n," and sometimes, though less often, the first apostrophe, writing it "n'." I even discussed the difficulty of pronouncing it, especially when not in combination with other words. As I wrote: "The best I can do is to place my tongue on the roof of my mouth just above my upper front teeth, open my mouth slightly, and grunt. Friends who hear me as I walk around unconsciously doing this (I am conscious as I walk around, but unconscious of what I am doing) say I sound like a hog with a stomach-ache. Probably they mean a hog that will wind up as the ham on a plate of ham 'n' eggs."

Another seemingly unpromising subject that I turned into a piece of humor and sold was the artichoke. I opened (the article, not the artichoke) with: "I sometimes wonder whether artichokes were meant to be eaten." Their spiny appearance, as well as the ominous "choke" in the name, might be meant as a warning. Exaggerating only a little, I described the curious, toothy way an artichoke is eaten and the appearance of one's plate when one has finished—with apparently more artichoke than before. The subject turned out to be a good one, though I no longer enjoy artichokes as I once did.

One of the rich areas of subject matter for humor is reminiscence. The idea is to write playfully about events of an earlier day that seemed serious then but in retrospect have a comic look about them, or can be made to look comic.

Everyone has material here, but it has to be handled in such a way as to seem true, or at least true to human nature, and yet somehow be lifted out of the commonplace.

Many writers of humor have capitalized on the adventures and misadventures of their childhood: school, the teacher, the first love affair (perhaps *with* the teacher and unknown to the teacher), stealing a smoke, taking care of pets, an inglorious camping trip, acting in a play, oddball relatives, and so on. This is the stuff of humorous articles and books by writers as various as Clarence Day, Max Shulman, James Thurber, Emily Kimbrough, Wolcott Gibbs, Stephen Leacock, Ruth McKenney, Sam Levenson, Jean Kerr, and, of course, Mark Twain. The tone varies from the playful-nostalgic to the wildly hilarious. The writer may make it frankly autobiographical, writing in the first person, or he may invent a character who is really himself.

In such writing, the writer must be willing to make fun of himself, make himself come out second best, or even third best. He must write about the mishaps, the failures, rather than the triumphs, and perhaps exaggerate a bit and make them seem worse than they really were. It helps to come of a large family and to have plenty of brothers and sisters and aunts and uncles and cousins to write about. Clarence Day could write of such a family, with a mixture of humor and affection, in *Life with Father,* and so could Frank B. Gilbreth, Jr., and Ernestine Gilbreth Carey in *Cheaper by the Dozen.*

I have been handicapped by being an only child and having only one uncle with whom I had any contact and only a few distant (both in relationship and in miles) cousins. But my small family contained enough odd characters to supply me with the material for numerous articles and several books. Take this description of my grandmother (my father's mother) in *Drug Store Days,* the story of my boyhood: "She was a large and in some ways handsome woman, with a Roman nose and a king-size (or queen-size) bust. The corseting of those days pulled her in at the middle and correspondingly spread her out above and below. Her bust formed a kind of ledge, on which she could place her glasses, her sewing materials, and a package of the large white mints which she ate incessantly." I needed only a few relatives such as my domineering grandmother, my dominated grandfather, and my ingenious Uncle Lester (ingenious in discovering ways of getting the family into trouble and keeping us impoverished) to flesh out a book that blended humor and nostalgia.

If you think about your family and yourself, especially going back to incidents of earlier years, you can probably find material such as I used in writing books like *Through Darkest Adolescence* and *My Life with Women,* as well as dozens of articles in magazines such as *Family Circle, Woman's Day, Parents' Magazine,* and *The Reader's Digest.* The older you get, the more past you have to reminisce about and dredge for humor. But you can also do this when you are fairly young. Even in your twenties you can experience what Wordsworth called "emotion recollected in tranquillity" by thinking back to your teens. The time gap need not be large, not more than a few years between present and past, for you to achieve that perspective that turns the tragic, or what seemed tragic, into the comic.

If you want to see what a first-rate writer of humor can do with a family incident recalled and recreated some years later, read James Thurber's "The Night the Bed Fell." It is one of the pieces in the "Reminiscence" section of *A Sub-*

treasury of American Humor, edited by E. B. White and Katharine S. White. Notice the simple, matter-of-fact, personal opening sentence: "I suppose that the high-water mark of my youth in Columbus, Ohio, was the night the bed fell on my father." After this straightforward beginning, it builds to a wild climax involving not only Thurber's father but a houseful of eccentric relatives. How much of the story is real and how much imagined is hard to tell, but the Thurber imagination, which, after all, created Walter Mitty, is plenty active.

However, you need not reminisce. You can probably find sufficient material in the present. Consider your office and your colleagues. Consider your car and traffic and parking. Consider the service station, the public library, the supermarket. Consider your house, your garden, your neighbors. You may be able to turn an irritation into a humorous article. You may offset an expense by the check you get for a fifteen-hundred-word piece about whatever caused the expense. I did precisely that, almost to the dollar, by writing an article about a burglary in our home and an embarrassing write-up of the incident in the local paper. Among the items listed as stolen, and dwelt upon at some length, were several cases of beer. . . .

I have long been annoyed by a tree in my neighbor's yard that showers me with leaves. The prevailing wind is such that the leaves drop into my neighbor's driveway, march up to the sidewalk, make a right-angle turn, and then scatter into hiding places in my front yard. Some slyly move on into our garage and, if I leave my car door open an instant too long, actually climb inside with me. I discharged some of my annoyance in an article I wrote and sold. The editor who bought it was so enthusiastic that I am sure he, too, has a tree next door that keeps him busy with a rake and a broom. I called my article "Leaf Me Alone."

These are some of the close-to-yourself subjects. Let me mention one other source of material that I have found useful in writing humor. That is the newspaper. The daily paper is a wonderful mirror of human activities, including many that are absurd or with a little twisting and exaggeration can be made absurd. S. J. Perelman frequently takes off from something he has spotted in the paper. Consider the item, "Baron Teviot of Burghclere, 33, who until his father's death Sunday was Charles John Kerr, plans to go back to work as a trainee supermarket checker." This was the seed that grew into Perelman's article, "Call Me Monty, and Grovel Freely," published in *The New Yorker*. Another news item, "Some people are literally allergic to work, according to a report submitted to an Italian medical conference," led Perelman to write "Five Little Biceps and How They Flew," which also found its way into *The New Yorker*.

I constantly search the newspaper for usable ideas. One item, pointing out that the first celebration of Thanksgiving was in Virginia, not Massachusetts, started me on a playful article, "Yes, Virginia, There Is a Thanksgiving," that I placed with *Family Weekly*. Another newspaper piece, saying that anyone who approaches a strange dog should do so with the back of the hand outstretched, was the basis of "Going to the Dog," which was published in "The Phoenix Nest" of the *Saturday Review*.

The newspaper is a wonderful source of ideas for all kinds of writing, and especially for humor. I commend it to you.

The material for humor is all around you. You haven't

far to look. Indeed the close-in material is frequently the best. Like the elbow, it is often overlooked.

But in writing humor, as in writing anything else, the material is less important than how you look at it and what you do with it.

CHAPTER THIRTEEN

Getting Technical

THERE are two ways of looking at any subject: the way of the serious writer and the way of the writer of humor. The writer of humor looks for the absurd, the incongruous, the inconsistent, the out of kilter, the ridiculous. If he was born with the right turn of mind, or if he has learned how to turn his mind the right way, he will find some or all of these elements in just about everything—especially himself.

As I sit in my study writing this, I look over my typewriter at a bookcase crammed with books. I have never before thought of this, but can I look at that bookcase in the humor writer's way? Can I find enough of the absurd and incongruous that I could write a funny piece about it? Of course I can. It is beginning to come now. . . . I have started to twist my already twisted mind a little more. I notice a book entitled *When Did It Happen?* Next to it is *Only Yesterday*. What messages I might get by looking over all of my books and noticing some strange juxtapositions! Perhaps someone is trying to tell me something. A little imagining, and I could be off on a Thurberesque piece of fantasy.

Once started, it is hard for me to leave my speculation about the books in that bookcase. I am beginning to wonder what explains that gap between two books. Did I lend a book to someone? What book? And to whom? Are there any books I myself have failed to return? Could I write a piece on "Kleptomaniacs I Have Known"? Did anyone ever burn his library card, a conscientious objector to reading? If I were honest about it, what books would I really want if I were marooned on a desert island? Why is it always a *desert* island? Don't they really mean a deserted island?

This is to illustrate the way a writer of humor approaches a subject, taking the offbeat view and looking for inconsistencies and absurdities. But this is only the beginning. Now, as he starts putting together words and sentences, comes his use of one or more of the techniques used to mine the humor out of the lode he has discovered. I am not sure whether the approach or attitude of the humor writer can be taught. But the techniques can be.

Here are some of the techniques that I have noticed in my reading of humor and that I use in my own writing:

1. *Exaggeration.* This is a basic and time-honored technique. Some think it a specialty of American writers of humor, perhaps forgetting Germany's Baron Munchausen. But Americans are good at it. It is what Mark Twain used in his tall tale, "The Celebrated Jumping Frog of Calaveras County." Instead of exaggeration of an event, an action, it may take the form of verbal exaggeration or hyperbole—

using unnecessarily big words, overstating—as in the writings of S. J. Perelman. Since it can easily run away with you and leave reality too far behind, it should be kept under control. Perelman uses it perfectly. So, though in a different way, does Robert Benchley.

Exaggeration is a weakness of mine. I sometimes exaggerate too much, go beyond the bounds of plausibility. But I have a valuable safety device or exaggeration checker in my home—my wife. She is especially sensitive to over-exaggeration, and when I try a new piece of writing on her and have gone too far, she lets me know. An instance is a chapter in *My Life with Women,* where I tell of an incident in college when our class went on a hiking trip to the mountains and I had a date with an athletic girl who was much stronger than I. She had bigger biceps and wider shoulders.

In the course of the hike I fell over the edge of a cliff, saved myself by clinging to a fortunately placed tree, and was pulled up by this muscular Amazon. So far, even with all the embellishments I am not quoting, the story seemed to me believable, though I had purposely exaggerated enough to lift it above the ordinary and give it touches of absurdity.

What my wife objected to was my saying that, since I had sprained an ankle, the girl carried me down the mountain over her shoulder, like a sack of potatoes. "That," she said, "is ridiculous."

Correct. It was the ridiculous that I was trying to achieve. Otherwise it wouldn't have been funny. Maybe I *did* overdo it. I have such trust in my wife's judgment that I pared down the episode, removing some of the wilder portions. But I also trust my own judgment, so I cut it down only a little. I still had myself being carried over the girl's shoulder, like a sack of potatoes. Fortunately I don't think my wife read the book after it was published.

2. *Understatement.* This is subtler, harder to sustain. It is like looking through the wrong end of a telescope. Try writing a story in which you have a character to whom everything large looks small, everything important seems trivial. Imagine an issue of the newspaper in which minor events are in the headlines and on the front page, while major happenings are tucked away in a small type on the back pages. Understatement in its way gets the same comic effect as overstatement, or exaggeration.

Reversal, involving the unexpected, can be used to good effect in humor. Think of the Cowardly Lion in *The Wizard of Oz.* Dry understatement is a feature of the Yankee cracker barrel philosophers, and the humor of Will Rogers. It is one of the devices of Thurber's imaginative but shrewd *Fables.* It can have a sharp edge to it but still be funny.

3. *Irony.* This, related to the above, is even subtler and sharper. Irony involves saying one thing and meaning another. Satirists, employing ridicule to attack the vices and follies of mankind, make much use of this. For a classic example, read Swift's caustic *A Modest Proposal.* Here the author suggests, with a straight face, that the poor people of Dublin fatten their infants until they are a year old and sell them to the rich for meat. "A child will make two dishes at an entertainment for friends," Swift writes, "and when the family dines alone, the fore or hind quarter will make a reasonable dish, and seasoned with a little pepper or salt will be very good boiled on the fourth day, especially in winter."

Outraged by conditions in Ireland, Swift wrote with a pen dipped in acid. His satire in *A Modest Proposal* contains little that could be called humor, unless it is humor of a gruesome sort.

I greatly admire Swift and have learned from him and imitated him. But when I write satire, I usually leaven it with humor, as Art Buchwald does. This way it is less likely to alienate the reader, and you have to keep your reader reading if you are to make your point. No matter how deep your convictions or how eager you are to convert others to your beliefs, you will probably get farther by writing with a smile than with a scowl.

I used irony, pushed to the point of absurdity, in an article called "How to Burn a Book," in which I told in detail how to do it and went on to suggest burning not only books but libraries, publishing houses, and finally, to get to the source—authors. There was some humor, I hope, in the exaggeration and absurdity as well as my light-hearted attitude. I might add that I got considerable mileage out of that piece. I sold it first to a library journal, then to a magazine in England, and later, as a reprint, to another magazine in the United States. Finally I worked it in as the last chapter of my *Going Around in Academic Circles*, a playful satire on higher education dedicated to "Socrates, the first professor to drink himself to death." The only time I have maintained irony for book length, trying to keep up the humor content despite the gruesomeness of the subject, was in *It All Started with Stones and Clubs*, a satire on the history of war and weaponry.

Irony is risky. It can be misunderstood. But it is effective in satire and can, if you keep your own sense of humor while writing it, be fun.

4. *Puns, word play.* Puns have been called the lowest form of humor. It makes a difference, though, whether they are your puns or someone else's. Charles Lamb, who was a great (that is, frequent) punster, wrote that "A pun is a pistol let off at the ear; not a feather to tickle the intellect." However, puns can be subtle and knowledgeable. Playing with words is, I think, indicative of one's love of language and perhaps of one's facility with it. You will find some skillful, highly original puns in the writing of James Thurber and S. J. Perelman, both of them word lovers.

But you must be careful with puns. Use them sparingly, always rigorously selecting only the best, as is done by a writer like Peter DeVries in his comic novels. Or, like Bennett Cerf, you might throw them about with such wild abandon that perhaps the good puns will outnumber the bad ones and the laughs will drown out the groans. In either case don't linger over them, don't stop to admire them yourself. Toss them off casually but appropriately and hurry on.

Humor is very personal and individual, often a matter of mood. The humor that delights one person repels another. The writer of humor must find the kind he likes most and writes best. Then he must work at it. Much depends on the nuances of meaning and connotation of words, which is one reason why humor requires revision and polish more than most kinds of writing.

My final suggestions are to read good models, get into a playful or quizzical mood, look closely at the people and things around you and perhaps into a mirror, and start hitting your typewriter keys. Humor is always in short supply. The world needs it.

And that includes editors, who have a special way of proving their sincerity. When they say they need humor, they mean it. They pay for it.